10 STEP
WATERCOLOUR

FLOWERS
AND PLANTS

Published in 2022 by Search Press Limited
Wellwood, North Farm Road
Tunbridge Wells
Kent TN2 3DR

This book is produced by
The Bright Press,
an imprint of the Quarto Group,
The Old Brewery, 6 Blundell Street,
London N7 9BH, United Kingdom.
T (0)20 7700 6700
www.QuartoKnows.com

ISBN: 978-1-80092-007-1
ebook ISBN: 978-1-80093-000-1

Publisher: James Evans
Editorial Director: Isheeta Mustafi
Art Director: James Lawrence
Managing Editor: Jacqui Sayers
Editor: Emily Angus
Project Editor: Anna Southgate
Designer: Emma Clayton

Printed and bound in China

MIX
Paper from
responsible sources
FSC® C016973
FSC
www.fsc.org

10 STEP WATERCOLOUR

FLOWERS AND PLANTS

PAINT 25 BEAUTIFULLY DETAILED FLOWERS IN 10 EASY STEPS

ELEANOR LONGHURST

Search Press

CONTENTS

1 GETTING STARTED

INTRODUCTION

Who doesn't love a beautiful bunch of flowers or a leafy houseplant? My flat is filled with them and I like to spend time among the wildflowers on my allotment.

Flowers are some of the first things you draw as a child, and my fascination with them has never stopped. I've always been intrigued by British wildflowers in particular, and wildflower illustrations form an integral part of my business, Little Paisley Designs, which I started in 2014.

My floral paintings have featured in different products, including embroidered patches and notebooks, and have been sent all over the world. I have enjoyed introducing British flora to a whole new audience, mixing illustrations of flora and fauna with colourful and modern patterns. I hope this book continues in the same vein.

My work focuses primarily on British nature, so it has been a delight to explore flowers and houseplants from further afield, to offer a really colourful mix of flora from around the world, in a variety of shapes and sizes. My paintings demonstrate the range of colours and techniques that can be achieved using watercolours – loose, flowing petals lend themselves so naturally to the medium. It has been lovely researching and painting these flowers and plants, among them some of my personal favourites. I hope you enjoy learning to paint them!

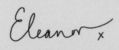

HOW TO USE THIS BOOK

Arranged in three chapters based on skill level, this book features twenty-five projects, each one showing you how to paint a plant or flower in ten steps. You can pick and choose the ones you would like to paint. If you are a beginner, however, it would be a good idea to start with one or two easy projects to build your confidence before moving on.

Useful tips offer advice on working methods and techniques.

Each project has a skill rating: easy, moderate or advanced.

Swatches show the colours you need to mix for each step.

Numbers beside the colour swatches
tell you which brush sizes to use.

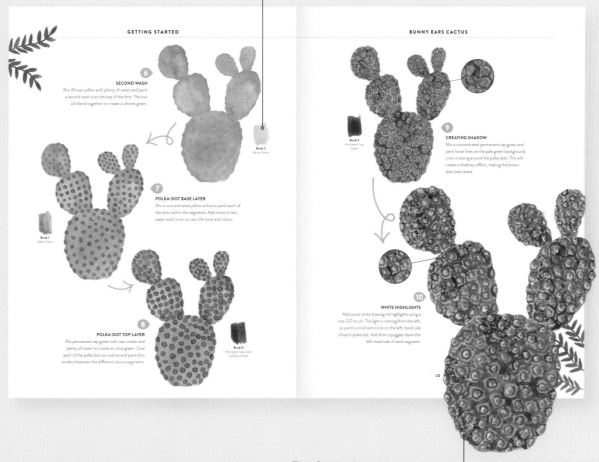

6

SECOND WASH
Mix Winsor yellow with plenty of water and paint
a second wash over the top of the first. The two
will blend together to create a vibrant green.

7

POLKA-DOT BASE LAYER
Mix a concentrated yellow ochre to paint each of
the dots within the segments. Add more or less
water each time, to vary the tone and colour.

Brush 1
Yellow Ochre

8

POLKA-DOT TOP LAYER
Mix permanent sap green with raw umber and
plenty of water to create an olive green. Give
each of the polka dots an outline and paint thin
borders between the different cactus segments.

Brush 0
Permanent Sap Green
and Raw Umber

Brush 2
Winsor Yellow

9

CREATING SHADOW
Mix a concentrated permanent sap green and
paint loose lines on the pale green background,
criss-crossing around the polka dots. This will
create a shadowy effect, making the brown
dots look raised.

Brush 2
Permanent Sap
Green

10

WHITE HIGHLIGHTS
Add some white drawing ink highlights using a
size 2/0 brush. The light is coming from the left,
so paint a small semicircle on the left-hand side
of each polka dot. Add short squiggles down the
left-hand side of each segment.

23

The finished painting serves as a
reference to guide you as you work.

USING WATERCOLOURS

All projects in this book use the same materials and work in the same way. Many of the steps use the same techniques no matter which plant or flower you are painting. Read through this section closely before starting a project and refer back to these pages if you need any reminders on which tools and techniques to use while working.

CHOOSING MATERIALS

Each plant or flower is painted on a sheet of A5 paper, using the same twenty-four-pan paint set and palette, and a range of brushes in five sizes.

PAPER

I use cold-pressed watercolour paper, as I have a particular affection for its hammered texture and ability to soak up the paint. If you prefer the grain of the paper not to show through in your paintings, opt for hot-pressed watercolour paper, which is smooth.

The size of paper I use measures around 15 x 21cm (5¾in x 8⅓in), and I prefer a good, heavyweight thickness (300gsm). It means you can paint on both sides without colour bleeding through, which is excellent for practising. My style of painting involves using more pigment and less water than traditional watercolour painting, and so the paper is less likely to warp.

PENCIL

I use a regular HB pencil to carry out all of the drawing stages in these projects, and a good-quality pencil sharpener to keep the tip pointed.

PAINTS

Watercolour paints come in sets containing small blocks of concentrated pigment called pans. I use a Winsor & Newton Professional Watercolour set with twenty-four half pans. The quality is far superior to anything else I have tried, and the pigments so rich. But they are rather pricey. If you are a beginner, a Winsor & Newton Cotman Watercolour set is a great entry-level option. The colour names I use in this book (see below) are found in the professional set, but I have included swatches of my mixes beside each step so you can create colours that best match them. As you become more skilled at painting with

| Lemon Yellow | Winsor Yellow | Aureolin | Winsor Orange | Winsor Red | Permanent Alizarin Crimson | Permanent Rose | Cerulean Blue |

| Winsor Violet | Winsor Blue | French Ultramarine | Prussian Blue | Indigo | Olive Green | Permanent Sap Green | Viridian |

| Yellow Ochre | Raw Sienna | Burnt Sienna | Raw Umber | Burnt Umber | Payne's Gray | Ivory Black | Chinese White |

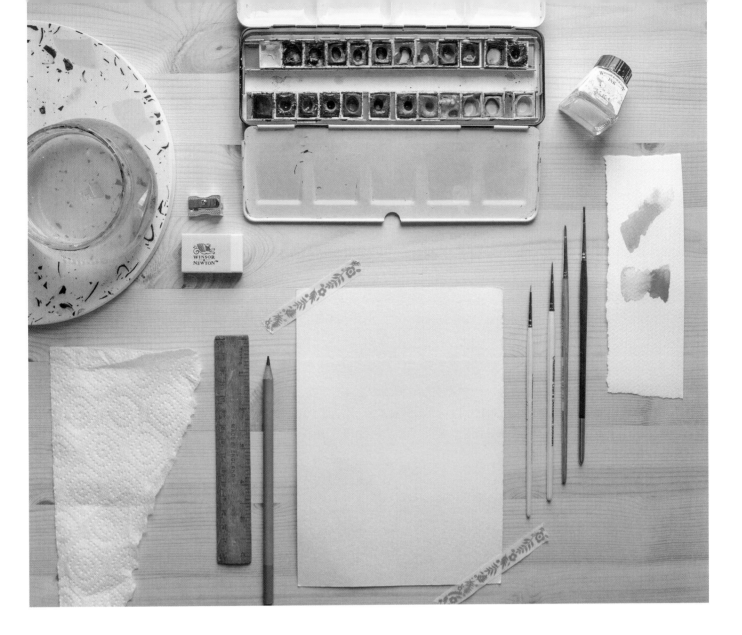

watercolours, it is worth investing in quality paints – you will use less pigment and they can last you a lifetime.

I like to finish my paintings with a layer of fine detail using white Winsor & Newton Drawing Ink. This is particularly good for creating highlights on the flower petals, to show where the light hits, and to add fine details at the end. As an alternative to the white drawing ink, you can mix Chinese white watercolour pigment with a little water to achieve the same results.

It is important to take care of your paint palette, to keep it looking its best. When you need to change colours, always clean your brush between dipping. If you accidentally mix colours within the pans and your yellow has green paint in it – this is easily done – just add a little water to the pan, and dab with a piece of paper towel until the paint pan is back to its original colour.

PAINTBRUSHES

I have used five brush sizes for the projects in this book, and prefer pointed round brushes because they are very flexible and allow for a wide range of brushstrokes. The brushes are Pro Arte Prolene brushes in sizes 2, 1 and 2/0, Pro Arte Masterstroke brushes in size 0, and Cass Art synthetic round brushes in size 000. All of the effects featured in the projects can be achieved using these.

Whichever brushes you choose to use, make sure you take care of them. Keep them clean and they will last. Once you have finished using a brush, do not leave it standing in water. This will make the paint on the handle splinter over time, and you will split the bristles. Instead, once you have finished with a colour, simply dip the brush in water, swill it around, dab with a paper towel and leave to dry on a new sheet of paper towel.

OTHER EQUIPMENT

There are several other pieces of equipment that you will find very useful. The first is an artist-quality eraser. This is important for removing pencil lines from your sketches without damaging the paper. When erasing pencil lines, always move your eraser in the same direction as the pencil lines and press lightly and slowly, keeping one hand firmly on the paper to hold it in place.

I always keep a large stack of paper towels on my desk, which I use for a wide range of purposes, including wiping colour off my brush, drying my brushes and dabbing my painting as I work. In this last role, the paper is not only invaluable when it comes to removing mistakes, but can be used to create a range of textured effects by dabbing away at a wet paint layer.

Another key piece of kit is a vessel for holding your water. I use an old glass jar. Make sure your vessel has a wide base so you cannot knock it over and is not so tall that you can lose your brush in it. Crucially, use a vessel made from clear glass or plastic so that you can see when you need to change the water. Do this frequently throughout a painting session, to keep your colour mixes bright and as you intend them.

WORKSPACE

Always try to paint in natural daylight. Your colours will look better, and you will be able to see what you are doing more clearly. If you cannot dedicate space to painting alone, clear some room on a desk or dining table and have everything you need within reach.

DRAWING TECHNIQUES

I start each project by drawing shapes that capture the basic form and position of the plant or flower. In most projects this is a series of teardrop and circle shapes that represent the different parts and their relative proportions. With these in place, I refine the outline and draw in all the details I want to paint – petal layers, leaf shapes and changes of colour.

I prefer my finished paintings to have only the faintest trace of pencil in them. Once I have an outline I like, I go over the lines again, pressing hard. Erasing the pencil slowly and carefully leaves me with a faint line and an indent that acts as an invisible border for the paint.

MIXING WATERCOLOURS

• Always use a clean palette to mix your colours.

• Your brush should always be wet. Even the most concentrated colour needs a wet brush in order to create fluid lines. Too little water will cause the pigment to run out, resulting in broken lines.

• Start with the lightest of two (or more) colours you plan to mix together. Add lots of water to your brush, dab this on an empty section of the paint palette, then sweep the brush over the first pan of dry colour. Add enough pigment to the water on the palette to make quite a concentrated colour. Clean your brush and sweep over the next pan of dry colour. Little by little add this, and other colours, to the first, until you have achieved the shade you want.

• Mix more paint than you think you will need, using a larger paintbrush than you plan to use. It can be difficult to replicate the exact shade if you need to mix more.

• Remember, you can always add more water to thin the paint mix, or more pigment to make the colour more concentrated.

• Keep a piece of scrap watercolour paper on your desk to test how different colours look before you apply them to your painting. I tend to use the smoother, hot-pressed watercolour paper for this.

• Once you are painting, if you add too much water, you can always dab at the paint lightly with a paper towel. This is much easier than having to stop your flow to add more water to the brush.

Tiny amount of water   A little water   More water   Lots of water   Tiny amount of paint   Paint after dabbing with a paper towel (right)

VARYING AMOUNTS OF WATER

You will see that I use quite concentrated colours. In fact, when I instruct you to use a 'concentrated' mix of any colour, this still has water blended in – just in tiny amounts. As you add more water, the colours you make become less and less opaque.

REFRESHING DRIED PAINT MIXES

Quite often, the same colour mix is used multiple times in a project – either returned to in a later step or mixed with other colours. If a colour dries between steps, refresh it by applying enough water to your brush to turn the mix back to wet paint. You may need to add more pigment, too.

BASIC WORKING METHODS

WORKING WET-ON-DRY

For the majority of projects in this book, the steps are painted using the wet-on-dry method. This means letting the paint dry before adding another layer of wet paint on top of, or next to, a painted section. This allows you to build layers of colour gradually, and to paint different colours beside each other without them bleeding into one another. It is important to let the paint dry between colours to keep the painting looking neat and to allow clear definition. Do not try to rush the process by using a hairdryer or popping the paper on a radiator, as this will cause the paint to run and the paper to warp.

WORKING WET-ON-WET

For some projects, you will apply wet paint on top of, or next to, a wet paint section so that the colours blend together. This is called the wet-on-wet method. It does not allow as much control, but can create some lovely soft textures. I usually work wet-on-wet in the first few steps of a painting, to create a blended base on which to add detail. The Swiss cheese plant project is a good example of this.

WORKING DRY-ON-DRY

Using a very concentrated paint on top of a dry layer introduces a more textured finish. I use this to create fine detail within the centre of flowers, or to add the fine white detail layer at the end of a project.

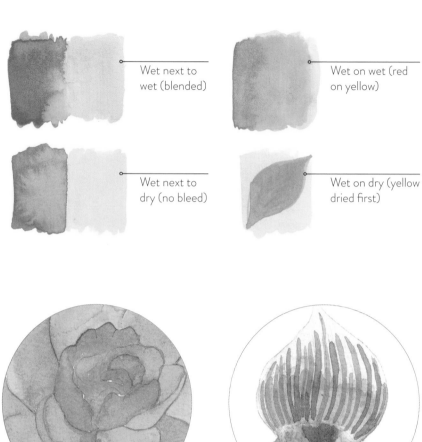

Wet next to wet (blended)

Wet on wet (red on yellow)

Wet next to dry (no bleed)

Wet on dry (yellow dried first)

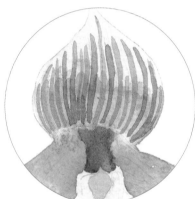

Wet-on-wet

Wet-on-dry

Wet-on-wet, with dabbing

Dry-on-dry

BRUSHSTROKES

I usually use the largest of my brushes (2 and 1) to apply the first washes of colour, and the smallest brush – 2/0 – for the finer details. You will find the appropriate brush sizes alongside the colour swatches that I give with each step.

You can achieve a wide variety of thicknesses with each brush, by varying the amount of pressure you place on it. Using scrap paper and paint with plenty of water, take some time to get to know the different strokes you can achieve. Tilting the brush at different angles allows you to create a range of effects. A thick brushstroke with a thin tapered end is easily achievable using a long, pointed brush, such as a size 2. Simply apply less pressure to the brush as the line progresses.

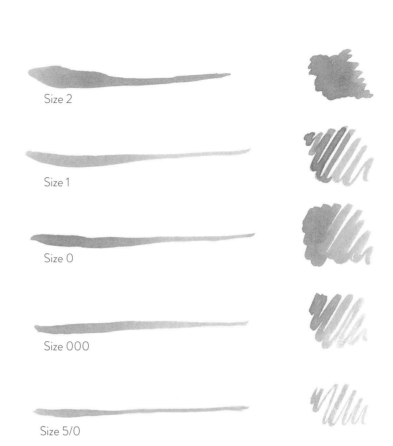

Size 2

Size 1

Size 0

Size 000

Size 5/0

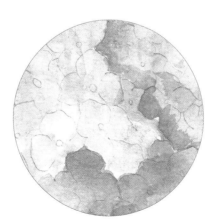

Larger brushes are best suited to washes and broader brushstrokes.

Small brushes can be fiddly at first, but are easy to correct if you make a mistake, as the marks are smaller.

USEFUL TECHNIQUES

I have used a wide range of techniques to capture the natural shapes and colours of the plants and flowers. Experiment with these methods and use them in different ways to create light and dark tones, to capture texture and to master three-dimensionality.

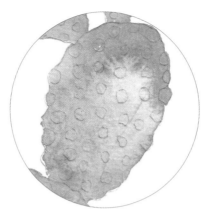

FIRST WASH

I tend to start a painting with a light wash as a base on which to build darker colours. I apply this using a size 2 brush and plenty of water. By varying the amount of pigment and/or water, I create a range of different tones. My bunny ears cactus is a good example of this.

LAYERING

Many steps involve building layers to create depth. I often layer washes of different colours to create one rich colour. For example, I might layer green and brown to create a deeper green. On the cornflower, I used different tones of the same colour to create depth.

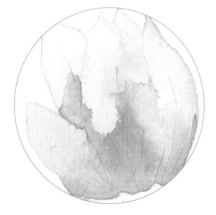

WET-ON-WET

For a few projects, including the magnolia and sweet pea, I really make use of the organic effects of applying wet paint on a water layer, letting the colours blend together beautifully. This can be quite tricky to control.

DABBING

Using a paper towel to dab away at layers of wet paint can create a range of tone within a painting, easily adding highlights without the use of white paint. You can use the same technique to remove paint if you make a mistake while painting.

FLORAL CONTOURS

The camellia, peony and rose have layers of delicate, curved petals. I draw smaller, tighter shapes at the centre and larger, looser shapes for outer petals. I use more pigment at the base of a petal, and more water towards the top for a lighter colour.

LEAF TONE

To create depth and tone in the leaves, I'll often paint a green wash, then add another colour, such as brown, to the mix and paint this over one half as a shadow. Choose one side as the light source and paint that side with white highlights, and the other with darker shadows.

FINE DETAIL

I always keep the finest details to the top two layers of a painting and use the smallest brush sizes to apply them. The passionflower, zebra plant, slipper orchid, cherry blossom and fritillary all have detailed patterns added with small brushes on the top layers.

WHITE HIGHLIGHTS

I like to add highlights using a small pointed paintbrush and either white drawing ink or a concentrated mix of Chinese white paint. It really makes the colours pop. I also add a watery final layer as a highlight along the 'light' side of a flower or leaf to show depth.

DISPLAYING YOUR WORK

Pop some washi tape on the corner of a finished painting for a quick way to display it on a wall. Several paintings from a collection of similar projects look great displayed this way. If you plan to mount and/or frame your finished paintings, bear in mind that you might want to use a larger paper size to allow for an even border all the way around the subject within the frame.

1

GETTING
STARTED

Here is a selection of projects that range in layout and scale. The drawing steps are simple and the fine details are easy to achieve. You will use the larger brush sizes for most of the work. The magnolia and mountain laurel projects introduce the wet-on-wet working method, and the bunny ears cactus is a good exercise on light and shade.

BUNNY EARS CACTUS

Opuntia microdasys

Also known as the polka-dot cactus, the oval, pad-like segments of this
desert species make it the perfect project to start with.

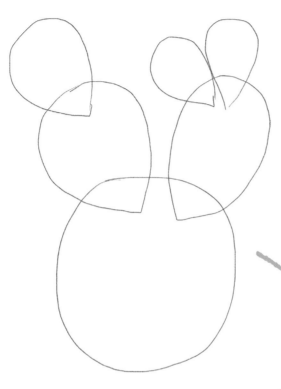

1

BASIC FORM

Using light pencil strokes, and following the
proportions and positions in my sketch, draw a
series of shapes that capture the cactus's basic
form. For reference, my sketch is 18cm tall by
13cm wide (7in x 5in), with the large, squarish
circle measuring 9cm (3½in) across.

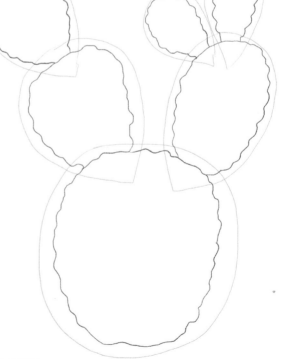

2

REFINED OUTLINE

Sketch a more accurate outline within your basic
shapes, using squiggled lines to render their
bumpy edges. You can add as many segments as
you like. Once happy with your outline, erase the
basic shapes.

3

PENCIL DETAILS

Using the final image as a reference, add more detail. Refine the outline and draw a series of polka dots within each of the segments, keeping the pattern fairly random. Go over the lines once more, pressing hard to create an indent to use as a border for the paint.

4

PENCIL IMPRESSION

Erase the pencil lines, leaving just the indent. If you prefer to keep a few marks, make sure you are happy for them to show through the paint.

5

FIRST WASH

Mix a very watery permanent sap green and use this to paint a wash over the shapes. Do not worry about leaving the dots blank, as the indent for each circle will show through the paint.

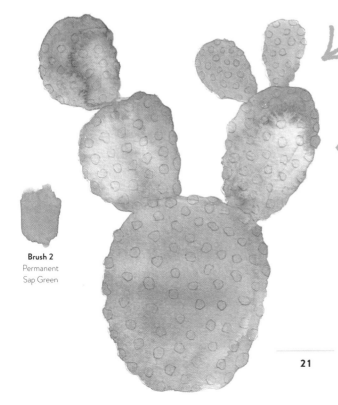

Brush 2
Permanent
Sap Green

21

6
SECOND WASH
Mix Winsor yellow with plenty of water and paint a second wash over the top of the first. The two will blend together to create a vibrant green.

Brush 2
Winsor Yellow

7
POLKA-DOT BASE LAYER
Mix a concentrated yellow ochre to paint each of the dots within the segments. Add more or less water each time, to vary the tone and colour.

Brush 1
Yellow Ochre

8
POLKA-DOT TOP LAYER
Mix permanent sap green with raw umber and plenty of water to create an olive green. Give each of the polka dots an outline and paint thin borders between the different cactus segments.

Brush 0
Permanent Sap Green
and Raw Umber

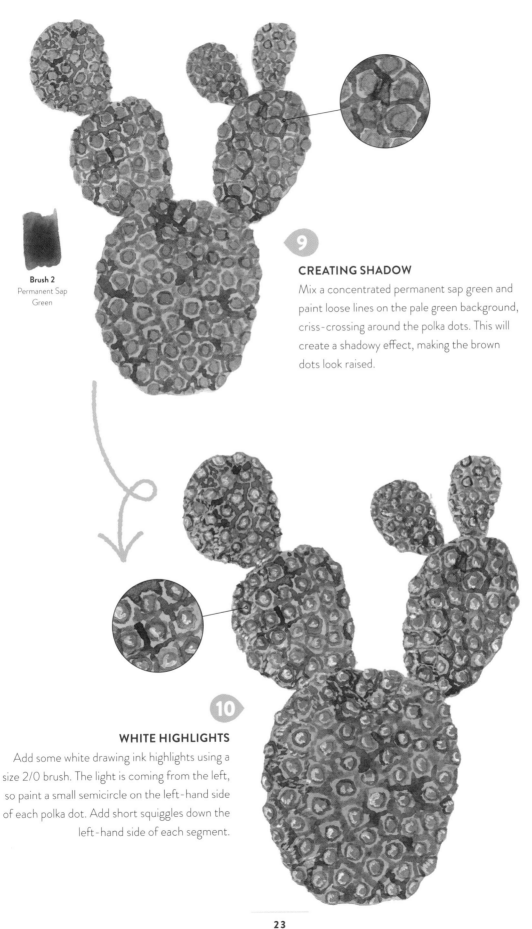

Brush 2
Permanent Sap
Green

9 CREATING SHADOW

Mix a concentrated permanent sap green and paint loose lines on the pale green background, criss-crossing around the polka dots. This will create a shadowy effect, making the brown dots look raised.

10 WHITE HIGHLIGHTS

Add some white drawing ink highlights using a size 2/0 brush. The light is coming from the left, so paint a small semicircle on the left-hand side of each polka dot. Add short squiggles down the left-hand side of each segment.

TRIOSTAR

Stromanthe sanguinea 'Triostar'

Native to the Amazon region of South America, this popular houseplant
has variegated leaves with deep pink undersides that show through.

1

BASIC FORM

Using light pencil strokes, and following the
proportions and positions in my sketch, draw a
series of shapes that capture the plant's basic
form. For reference, my sketch is 19cm tall by
13.5cm wide (7½in x 5⅓in), with the largest
teardrop shape measuring around 13cm x 5cm
(5in x 2in).

2

REFINED OUTLINE

Sketch a more accurate outline within your basic
shapes. Notice how the leaves all radiate out
from the centre, overlapping each other. Vary
the sizes of the leaves. Once happy with your
outline, erase the basic shapes.

3

PENCIL DETAILS

Using the final image as a reference, refine the leaves and draw in their central veins. Use a series of wavy lines to mark the changes of colour. Keep them organic and asymmetrical. Go over the lines once more, pressing hard to create an indent to use as a border for the paint.

4

PENCIL IMPRESSION

Erase the pencil lines, leaving just the indent. If you prefer to keep a few marks, make sure you are happy for them to show through the paint.

Allow each leaf to dry before painting the one next to it so that the colours do not blend into each other.

Brush 2
Chinese White, Lemon
Yellow, Permanent Rose

5

FIRST WASH

Mix Chinese white, lemon yellow and permanent rose with plenty of water. Wash this over the outer edges of the leaves, keeping the central sections blank. Vary the colour ratios to create a range of pink and yellow tones.

6

SECOND WASH

Add a drop of yellow ochre and plenty of water to the first wash mix. Paint the base of each leaf, pulling the colour up the leaf slightly in loose, flowing lines. Watch the colours blend into one another. Dab the paint with a paper towel if the new colour looks too dark.

Brush 2
Chinese White, Lemon Yellow, Permanent Rose, Yellow Ochre

Brush 2
Permanent Sap Green

7

VARIEGATED BASE LAYER

Mix a pale, watery permanent sap green and use this to paint a wash over the central section of each leaf.

8

BUILDING COLOUR

Make a concentrated viridian and permanent sap green mix and use this to paint the central vein on each leaf. Paint a few flowing lines that radiate out from the central vein, but without completely covering the pale green base layer.

Brush 2
Viridian and Permanent Sap Green

26

Brush 2
Viridian, Permanent Sap
Green, Indigo

*Switch to a size 0
brush if you would
like to add finer line
details at this stage.*

9

CREATING DEPTH

Mix some indigo and just a little water into the
dark green mix to create a deep inky green. Add
a few lines of this, again radiating out from the
central veins. Keep them random to create a
loose pattern.

Brush 2
Chinese White, Lemon
Yellow, Permanent Rose,
Yellow Ochre

10

FINISHING TOUCHES

Add some white drawing ink highlights using a
size 0 brush. Draw long lines over the leaves, to
pick out the natural contours. Using the Step 6
mix, paint a watery wash over the edges of the
lower leaves, leaving the top two leaves intact.

FIELD POPPY

Papaver rhoeas

Bringing a blaze of red to open fields and meadowland in summer, these fragile, short-lived blooms have become a symbol of remembrance.

1

BASIC FORM

Using light pencil strokes, and following the proportions and positions in my sketch, draw a series of shapes that capture the poppy's basic form. For reference, my sketch is 18cm tall by 13cm wide (7in x 5in), with the main circle shape measuring 9cm (3½in) across.

2

REFINED OUTLINE

Sketch a more accurate outline within your basic shapes. Notice how the petals have loose, flowing edges, while the leaves are more featherlike. Draw in the bud and join the shapes together with a long, flowing stem. Once happy with your outline, erase the basic shapes.

3 PENCIL DETAILS

Using the final image as a reference, refine the edges of the petals and add detail to the inside of the flower. Draw a central vein on each leaf. Go over the lines once more, pressing hard to create an indent to use as a border for the paint.

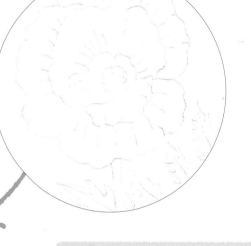

4 PENCIL IMPRESSION

Erase the pencil lines, leaving just the indent. If you prefer to keep a few marks, make sure you are happy for them to show through the paint.

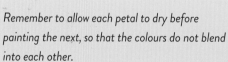

Remember to allow each petal to dry before painting the next, so that the colours do not blend into each other.

Brush 2
Winsor Red, Winsor Orange, Burnt Sienna

5 FIRST WASH

Mix Winsor red, Winsor orange and burnt sienna with plenty of water and paint a wash over the main petals and the bud. Starting at the centre of the flower, add more water as you paint outwards to vary the tone.

SECOND WASH

Make a fairly concentrated mix of permanent alizarin crimson and burnt sienna and paint the base of each petal and the lines that divide them. Paint just the left-hand side of the bud.

Brush 2
Permanent Alizarin Crimson and Burnt Sienna

Brush 2
Burnt Sienna and Payne's Gray

Brush 0
Permanent Alizarin Crimson

CREATING DEPTH

Mix burnt sienna and Payne's gray to create a deep brown for the outer circle at the flower's centre. Use a concentrated permanent alizarin crimson to paint over the indented lines at the base of each petal and on the bud.

LEAF COLOUR

Mix a concentrated permanent sap green and yellow ochre and paint the poppy's centre. Add more water to paint the leaves. Trace each central vein, adding more water so the colour flows outwards, and using your brush to push the paint into each point. Paint the top of the bud.

Brush 1
Permanent Sap Green and Yellow Ochre

Brush 1 & 0
Permanent Sap Green
and Burnt Umber

9 FINER DETAILS

Mix a concentrated olive green using permanent
sap green and burnt umber. Paint the stem.
Switch to a size 0 brush and paint a series of lines
radiating around the edge of the flower's central
circle. Paint over the central vein of each leaf.

10 WHITE HIGHLIGHTS

Add some white drawing ink highlights using a
size 2/0 brush. Trace the central vein of each leaf
and add thin, curved lines on each of the petals.
Paint a series of dots and dashes on the brown
section at the poppy's centre.

PANSY

Viola tricolor

The cheerful pansy is one of the first plants to flower in spring, emerging in a variety of colours. Use the steps here to paint a colourway of your choice.

1

BASIC FORM

Using light pencil strokes, and following the proportions and positions in my sketch, draw a series of shapes that capture the pansy's basic form. For reference, my sketch is 15cm tall by 12cm wide (6in x 4¾in), with each of the large ovals measuring 8cm x 6.5cm (3in x 2½in).

2

REFINED OUTLINE

Sketch a more accurate outline within your basic shapes. Each flower has four flat, overlapping petals and a triangular centre. The leaves are quite squat, with rounded bumpy edges. Once happy with your outline, erase the basic shapes.

3 PENCIL DETAILS

Using the final image as a reference, add more detail, marking out different areas of colour. Draw a central vein on each leaf, with shorter veins fanning out either side. Go over the lines once more, pressing hard to create an indent to use as a border for the paint.

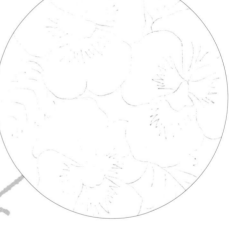

4 PENCIL IMPRESSION

Erase the pencil lines, leaving just the indent. If you prefer to keep a few marks, make sure you are happy for them to show through the paint.

Brush 2
Cerulean Blue,
Prussian Blue,
Permanent Rose

5 FIRST WASH

Mix cerulean blue, Prussian blue and permanent rose with plenty of water and paint the top section of each petal. This should be quite a watery wash, to let the colours blend together. Allowing each petal to dry before you paint the next will help you retain the shapes.

Be sure to leave a white border between this new colour and the pale purple of the first wash. Keep the centres white, too.

 6

DARKER DETAILS

Mix a concentrated indigo and Winsor violet and paint just the bases of the three lower petals on each flower. Switch to the size 2/0 brush to paint a few lines radiating out from the centre and reaching into the pale purple.

Brush 1 & 2/0
Indigo and
Winsor Violet

Brush 1
Aureolin

7

BRIGHT CENTRES

Paint the central triangular section of each flower with a concentrated aureolin mix.

8

LEAF COLOUR

Mix permanent sap green and indigo to create a deep green. Add plenty of water and paint each of the leaves, filling the shapes completely.

Brush 2
Permanent Sap
Green and Indigo

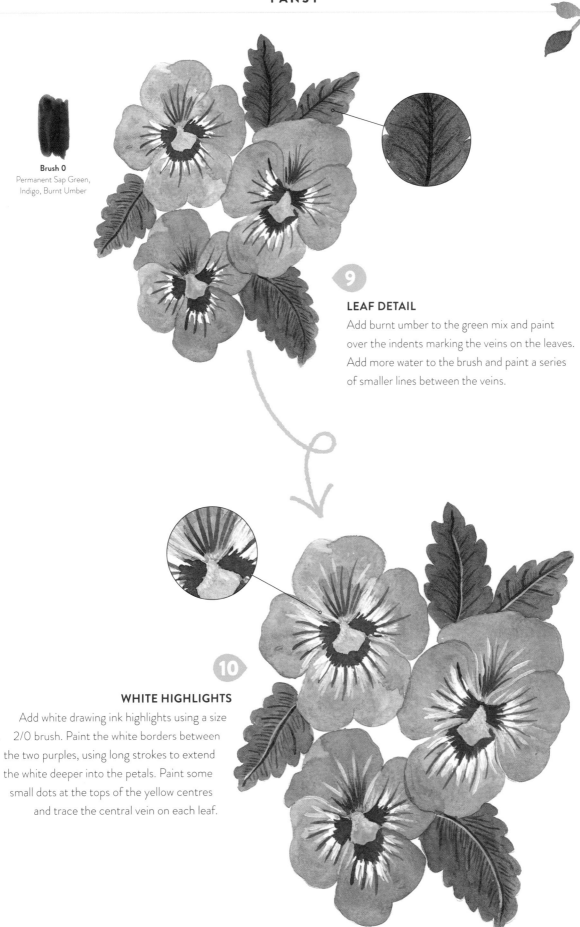

Brush 0
Permanent Sap Green,
Indigo, Burnt Umber

9

LEAF DETAIL

Add burnt umber to the green mix and paint over the indents marking the veins on the leaves. Add more water to the brush and paint a series of smaller lines between the veins.

10

WHITE HIGHLIGHTS

Add white drawing ink highlights using a size 2/0 brush. Paint the white borders between the two purples, using long strokes to extend the white deeper into the petals. Paint some small dots at the tops of the yellow centres and trace the central vein on each leaf.

CHERRY BLOSSOM

Prunus serrulata

Cherry blossom is associated with Japan, where it has great cultural significance.
The shortlived flowers symbolize the fleeting nature of existence.

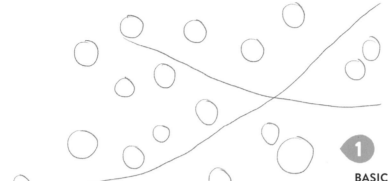

Vary the size of your circles, as the small ones will be unopened buds.

1

BASIC FORM

Using light pencil strokes, and following the proportions and positions in my sketch, draw the basic form of the blossom. For reference, my two twigs measure 20cm (8in) and 13cm (5in).

2

REFINED OUTLINE

Sketch a more accurate outline within your basic shapes. Draw each of the twigs fully and add petals to most of the flowers, varying their positions. Leave a few small unopened buds. Once happy with your outline, erase the basic shapes.

3 PENCIL DETAILS

Draw small circles for the centres of the flowers, and a series of lines radiating out into the petals. Go over the lines once more, pressing hard to create an indent to use as a border for the paint.

4 PENCIL IMPRESSION

Erase the pencil lines, leaving just the indent. If you prefer to keep a few marks, make sure you are happy for them to show through the paint.

The yellow and pink pigments may separate a little as they dry, adding to the delicate charm of the blossom.

Brush 2
Permanent Rose,
Chinese White,
Lemon Yellow

5 PETAL COLOUR

Mix permanent rose and Chinese white with a small amount of lemon yellow and plenty of water. Paint each of the petals and the buds using a thin wash so that you can still see the indents showing through.

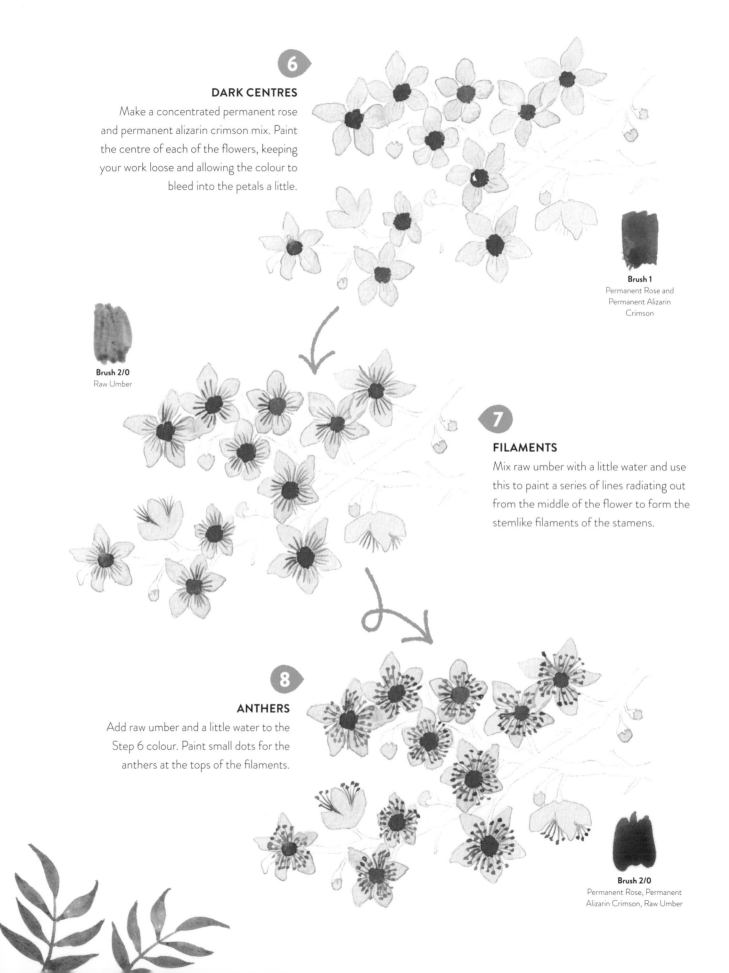

6

DARK CENTRES

Make a concentrated permanent rose and permanent alizarin crimson mix. Paint the centre of each of the flowers, keeping your work loose and allowing the colour to bleed into the petals a little.

Brush 1
Permanent Rose and Permanent Alizarin Crimson

Brush 2/0
Raw Umber

7

FILAMENTS

Mix raw umber with a little water and use this to paint a series of lines radiating out from the middle of the flower to form the stemlike filaments of the stamens.

8

ANTHERS

Add raw umber and a little water to the Step 6 colour. Paint small dots for the anthers at the tops of the filaments.

Brush 2/0
Permanent Rose, Permanent Alizarin Crimson, Raw Umber

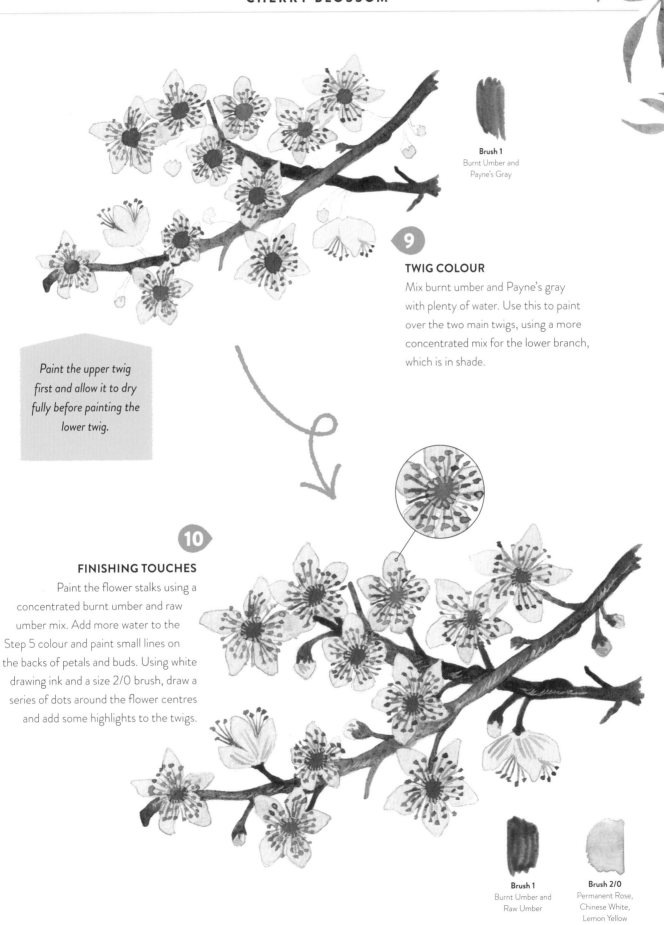

Brush 1
Burnt Umber and
Payne's Gray

9

TWIG COLOUR

Mix burnt umber and Payne's gray
with plenty of water. Use this to paint
over the two main twigs, using a more
concentrated mix for the lower branch,
which is in shade.

*Paint the upper twig
first and allow it to dry
fully before painting the
lower twig.*

10

FINISHING TOUCHES

Paint the flower stalks using a
concentrated burnt umber and raw
umber mix. Add more water to the
Step 5 colour and paint small lines on
the backs of petals and buds. Using white
drawing ink and a size 2/0 brush, draw a
series of dots around the flower centres
and add some highlights to the twigs.

Brush 1
Burnt Umber and
Raw Umber

Brush 2/0
Permanent Rose,
Chinese White,
Lemon Yellow

MAGNOLIA

Magnolia x soulangeana

This species of magnolia bears flowers before any leaves start to grow.
The large, tulip-shaped white flowers are flushed with pink or purple at the base.

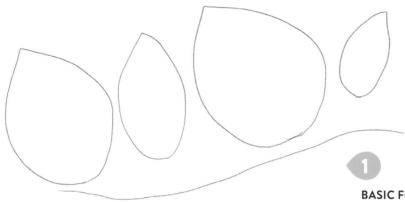

BASIC FORM

Using light pencil strokes, and following
the proportions and positions in my
sketch, draw a series of shapes that
capture the basic form of the branch.
For reference, my sketch is 20cm wide
by 12cm tall (7¾in x 4¾in), with the
largest teardrop shape measuring
6cm x 7cm (2⅓in x 2¾in).

REFINED OUTLINE

Sketch a more accurate outline
within your basic shapes. Notice how
the larger flowers are composed of
several petals folded over each other.
Make the branch bumpy in parts,
with sprigs and small leaves coming off
above and below.

3 PENCIL DETAILS

Using the final image as a reference, add more detail in the petals, keeping your lines nice and loose. Go over the lines once more, pressing hard to create an indent to use as a border for the paint.

4 PENCIL IMPRESSION

Erase the pencil lines, leaving just the indent. If you prefer to keep a few marks, make sure you are happy for them to show through the paint.

Brush 2
Permanent Rose,
Chinese White,
Lemon Yellow

5 FIRST WASH

Mix permanent rose, Chinese white and lemon yellow with plenty of water to make a pale pink wash. Paint each of the flowers, working in an upward motion from the base to the tips of the petals.

6

SECOND WASH

Using less water, add a drop of Prussian blue and more permanent rose to the first wash. Use a clean brush to wash water over the base of each flower. Add the new colour from the base upwards, so that it bleeds into the water, blending with the paler pink in a beautiful, organic way.

Brush 2
Prussian Blue and
Permanent Rose

This step uses the wet-on-wet method. If the colour looks too dark, dab it gently with a paper towel.

7

FLORAL CONTOURS

Add a drop of yellow ochre and lots of water to the Step 6 colour. Paint a series of thin lines that follow the contours of each petal, starting at the base of each flower and fading as they get near the top.

Brush 0
Prussian Blue,
Permanent Rose,
Yellow Ochre

8

LEAF COLOUR

Mix lemon yellow and permanent sap green with plenty of water. Paint the short flower stems and the buds and small leaves coming off the branch.

Brush 2
Lemon Yellow and
Permanent Sap Green

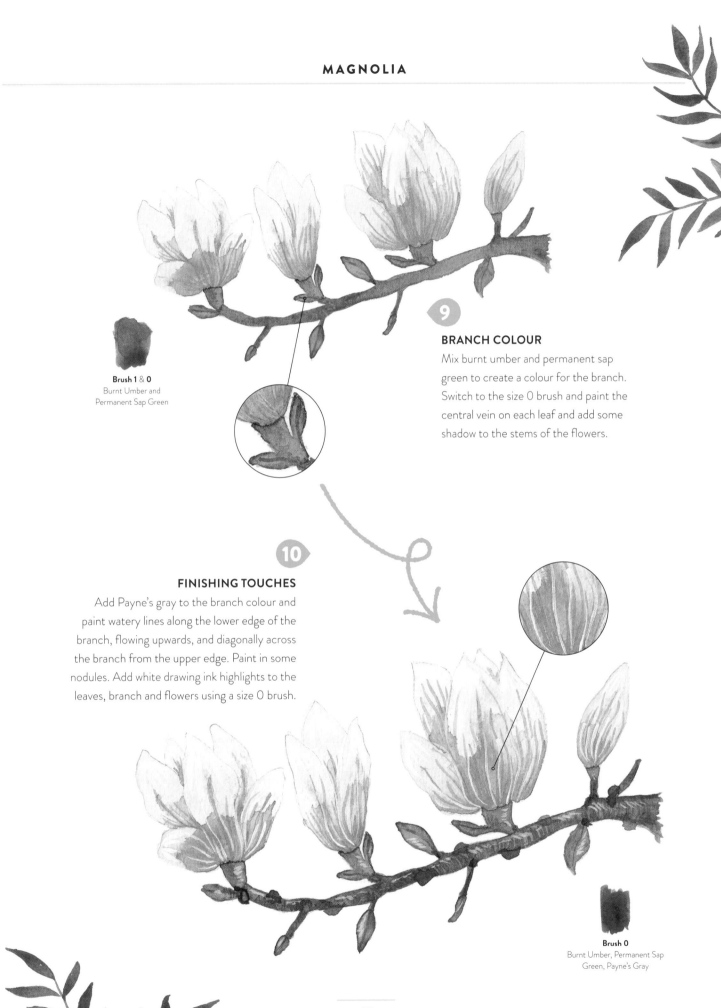

Brush 1 & 0
Burnt Umber and
Permanent Sap Green

9
BRANCH COLOUR

Mix burnt umber and permanent sap
green to create a colour for the branch.
Switch to the size 0 brush and paint the
central vein on each leaf and add some
shadow to the stems of the flowers.

10
FINISHING TOUCHES

Add Payne's gray to the branch colour and
paint watery lines along the lower edge of the
branch, flowing upwards, and diagonally across
the branch from the upper edge. Paint in some
nodules. Add white drawing ink highlights to the
leaves, branch and flowers using a size 0 brush.

Brush 0
Burnt Umber, Permanent Sap
Green, Payne's Gray

MAIDENHAIR FERN

Adiantum raddianum

There are around 200 species of maidenhair fern, all with delicate green fronds.
This one, the delta maidenhair fern, is a popular houseplant.

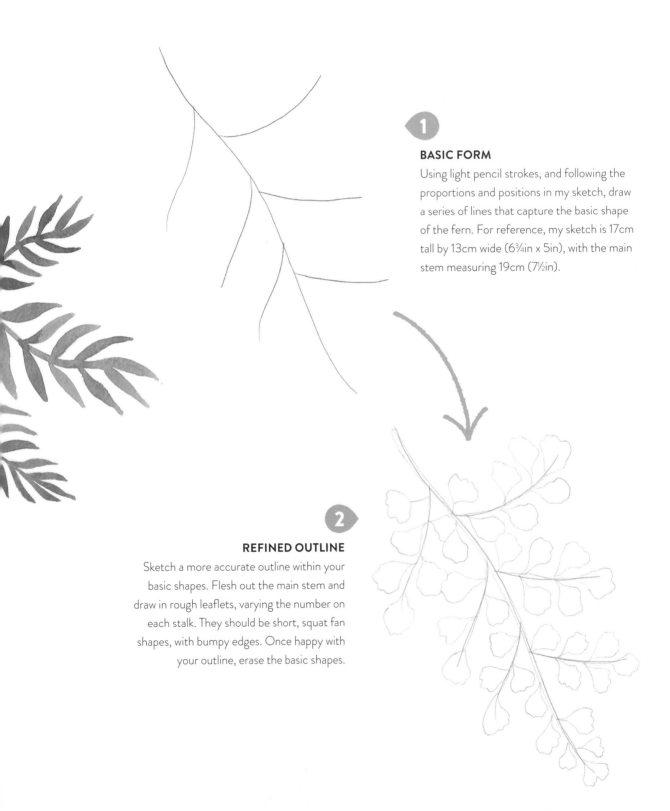

1

BASIC FORM

Using light pencil strokes, and following the proportions and positions in my sketch, draw a series of lines that capture the basic shape of the fern. For reference, my sketch is 17cm tall by 13cm wide (6¾in x 5in), with the main stem measuring 19cm (7½in).

2

REFINED OUTLINE

Sketch a more accurate outline within your basic shapes. Flesh out the main stem and draw in rough leaflets, varying the number on each stalk. They should be short, squat fan shapes, with bumpy edges. Once happy with your outline, erase the basic shapes.

 3

PENCIL DETAILS

Add more detail, refining the shapes of the leaflets. Draw lines fanning out across the width of each leaflet. Go over the lines once more, pressing hard to create an indent to use as a border for the paint.

 4

PENCIL IMPRESSION

Erase the pencil lines, leaving just the indent. If you prefer to keep a few marks, make sure you are happy for them to show through the paint.

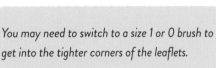

You may need to switch to a size 1 or 0 brush to get into the tighter corners of the leaflets.

 5

FIRST WASH

Create a watery yellow ochre and permanent sap green mix and paint a very thin layer over the leaflets. Do not worry if there is more or less water here and there – this adds to the organic nature of watercolours and stops the painting looking flat.

Brush 2
Yellow Ochre and
Permanent Sap Green

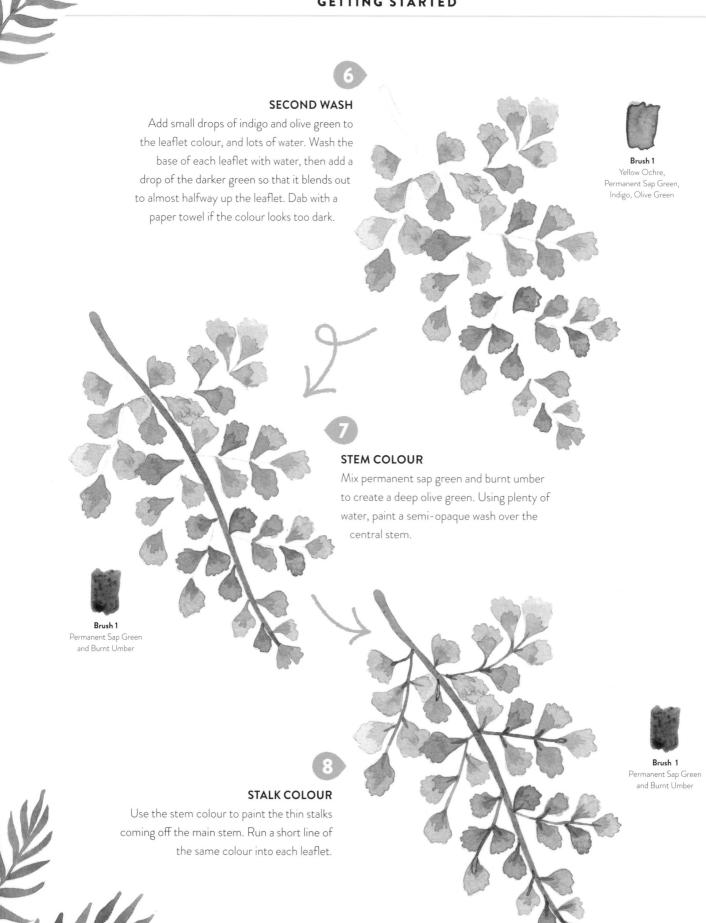

6

SECOND WASH

Add small drops of indigo and olive green to the leaflet colour, and lots of water. Wash the base of each leaflet with water, then add a drop of the darker green so that it blends out to almost halfway up the leaflet. Dab with a paper towel if the colour looks too dark.

Brush 1
Yellow Ochre,
Permanent Sap Green,
Indigo, Olive Green

7

STEM COLOUR

Mix permanent sap green and burnt umber to create a deep olive green. Using plenty of water, paint a semi-opaque wash over the central stem.

Brush 1
Permanent Sap Green
and Burnt Umber

8

STALK COLOUR

Use the stem colour to paint the thin stalks coming off the main stem. Run a short line of the same colour into each leaflet.

Brush 1
Permanent Sap Green
and Burnt Umber

9

FINE DETAILS

Add plenty of water to the stem colour and paint the lines fanning out across the width of each leaflet. Make sure there is plenty of water on your brush and it is not dragging on the page.

Brush 2/0
Permanent Sap Green and Burnt Umber

Remember, you can use Chinese white to add the highlights. This will enable you to make a more watery mix and therefore achieve greater transparency.

10

WHITE HIGHLIGHTS

Add white drawing ink highlights using a size 2/0 brush. Trace the lines fanning out across each leaflet and run a faint line of white down the main stem.

MOUNTAIN LAUREL

Kalmia latifolia

This final project of the chapter presents the challenge of setting the fragile-looking bell-shaped flowers and hot pink crinkled buds against glossy green leaves.

1

BASIC FORM

Using light pencil strokes, and following the proportions and positions in my sketch, draw a series of shapes that capture the basic form of the flowers. For reference, my sketch is 17cm tall by 13cm wide (6¾in x 5in), with the two largest circles measuring 5cm (2in) across.

2

REFINED OUTLINE

Sketch a more accurate outline within your basic shapes. Notice how the leaves are long and thin with pointed tips, while the flowers are squarish with five petals. Turn the circles into buds and draw in the stems. Once happy with your outline, erase the basic shapes.

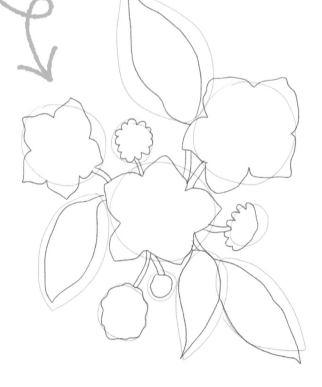

3

PENCIL DETAILS

Using the final image as a reference, add more detail to mark changes of colour in the flowers. For the crinkled buds, draw a series of thin lines around a central circle. Draw a central vein on each leaf. Go over the lines once more, pressing hard to create an indent to use as a border for the paint.

4

PENCIL IMPRESSION

Erase the pencil lines, leaving just the indent. If you prefer to keep a few marks, make sure you are happy for them to show through the paint.

Brush 1
Aureolin, Permanent
Rose, Chinese White

5

PALE PINK WASH

Mix aureolin, permanent rose and Chinese white with lots of water. Paint the outer edges of the three main flowers. This layer should be quite watery and pale.

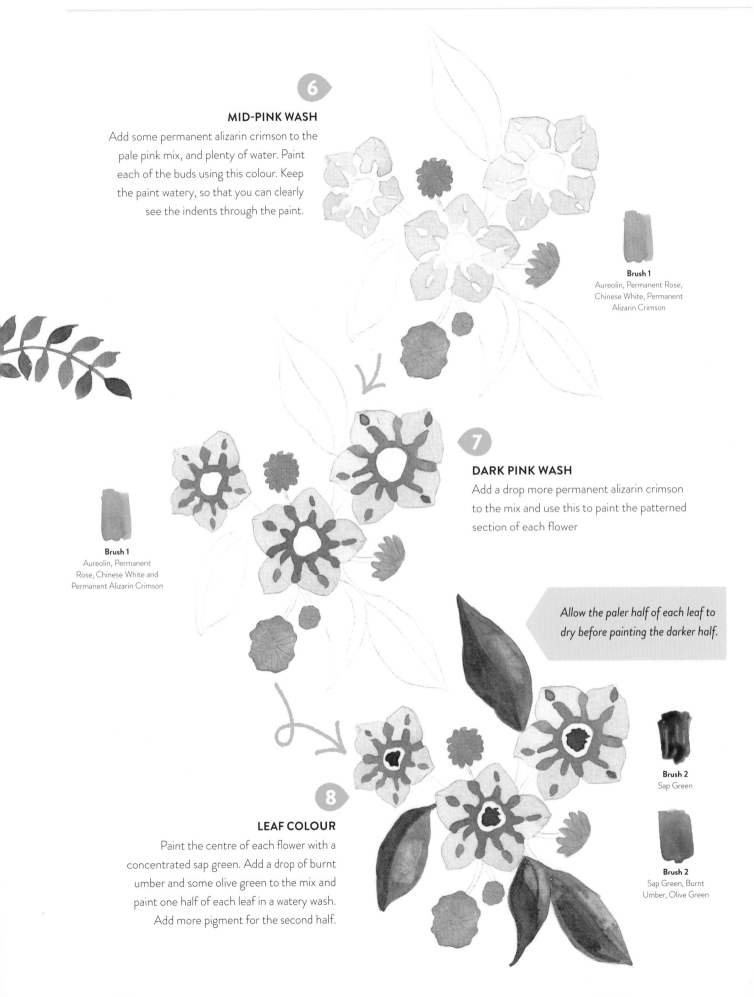

6

MID-PINK WASH

Add some permanent alizarin crimson to the pale pink mix, and plenty of water. Paint each of the buds using this colour. Keep the paint watery, so that you can clearly see the indents through the paint.

Brush 1
Aureolin, Permanent Rose, Chinese White, Permanent Alizarin Crimson

7

DARK PINK WASH

Add a drop more permanent alizarin crimson to the mix and use this to paint the patterned section of each flower

Brush 1
Aureolin, Permanent Rose, Chinese White and Permanent Alizarin Crimson

Allow the paler half of each leaf to dry before painting the darker half.

Brush 2
Sap Green

8

LEAF COLOUR

Paint the centre of each flower with a concentrated sap green. Add a drop of burnt umber and some olive green to the mix and paint one half of each leaf in a watery wash. Add more pigment for the second half.

Brush 2
Sap Green, Burnt Umber, Olive Green

Brush 0
Sap Green, Burnt
Umber, Olive Green

9 LEAF DETAIL

Add lots more burnt umber to the leaf mix
to make a darker olive green shade. Carefully
paint the thin stalks joining the flowers
and leaves. Trace the central vein running
through each leaf.

Brush 1
Aureolin, Permanent Rose,
Chinese White, Permanent
Alizarin Crimson

10 FINISHING TOUCHES

Using the Step 7 wash with plenty of water,
paint in some shadow areas where the petals
overlap and on the left-hand side of each bud.
Using white drawing ink, draw a series of lines
radiating out from the centre of each flower.
Trace the indents on the buds and the central
vein on each leaf.

2

BUILDING CONFIDENCE

The projects in this section have more complex drawing steps and some intricate arrangements. A number involve groups of flowers, while others, such as the peony and camellia, have many detailed layers. The projects build on light and shade and have more fine detail. You will explore the wet-on-wet method more with the sweet pea project.

ROSE

Rosa 'Ausbord'

Also known as the Jekyll Rose, after the renowned garden designer Gertrude Jekyll, this flower has double layers of petals that vary in hue from peach to glorious pink.

1

BASIC FORM

Using light pencil strokes, and following the proportions and positions in my sketch, draw a series of shapes that capture the rose's basic form. For reference, my sketch is 19cm tall by 14.5cm wide (7½in x 5¾in), with the large circle measuring 10cm (4in) across.

2

REFINED OUTLINE

Sketch a more accurate outline within your basic shapes, drawing in the larger rose petals. Give shape to the leaves, adding the central vein, and flesh out the bud. Join the leaves and flower together with a series of stems. Once happy with your outline, erase the basic shapes.

Skill Rating
MODERATE

3 PENCIL DETAILS

Using the final image as a reference, add some detail. Give shape to the petals, to capture a more three-dimensional perspective. Go over the lines once more, pressing hard to create an indent to use as a border for the paint.

4 PENCIL IMPRESSION

Erase the pencil lines, leaving just the indent. If you prefer to keep a few marks, make sure you are happy for them to show through the paint.

5 FIRST WASH

Mix aureolin, permanent rose and Winsor red, keeping it quite dilute. Painting from the centre of the flower, draw the brushstrokes out towards each petal edge. Add more pigment nearer the tops of the petals, and let it bleed into the watery layer. Paint the same colour over the bud.

Brush 2
Aureolin, Permanent
Rose, Winsor Red

Brush 1
Aureolin and
Permanent Rose

6

SECOND WASH

Mix aureolin and permanent rose with plenty
of water. Paint a series of curves on the inner
petals, following their form. On the larger petals,
paint vertical strokes and blend them in. Add
some of the orange tint to the underside of a few
petals, to show they are in shadow.

Brush 1
Sap Green and
Prussian Blue

7

LEAF COLOUR

Mix sap green with a little Prussian blue to make
a deep green. Fill the leaves with this colour,
painting in a diagonal direction. Trace the central
vein on each leaf.

8

STEM COLOUR

Mix sap green and a little burnt sienna. Paint
each stem, working in one long, flowing line for
each section. Once more, trace the central vein
on each leaf.

Brush 1
Sap Green and
Burnt Sienna

Brush 0
Sap Green and
Burnt Sienna

Brush 0
Permanent Rose

9

FINER DETAILS

Mix permanent rose with lots of water and paint the outer edges of the petals. Then, using a mix of sap green and burnt sienna, paint the shorter veins on the leaves. Wash lots of water over the top to blend the paint layers.

10

ROSY HIGHLIGHTS

Mix a tiny amount of permanent rose with lots of Chinese white and water. Add some detail along the petals to create highlights. Follow the curves of the petals. Use the same colour to trace the central vein of each leaf.

Brush 0
Permanent Rose
and Chinese White

SNAKE'S HEAD FRITILLARY

Fritillaria meleagris

With its delicate checkerboard-patterned petals, it's easy to see why this member of the lily family is also known as the chess flower.

There's something aesthetically pleasing about grouping objects in threes, so I've chosen to draw three buds here.

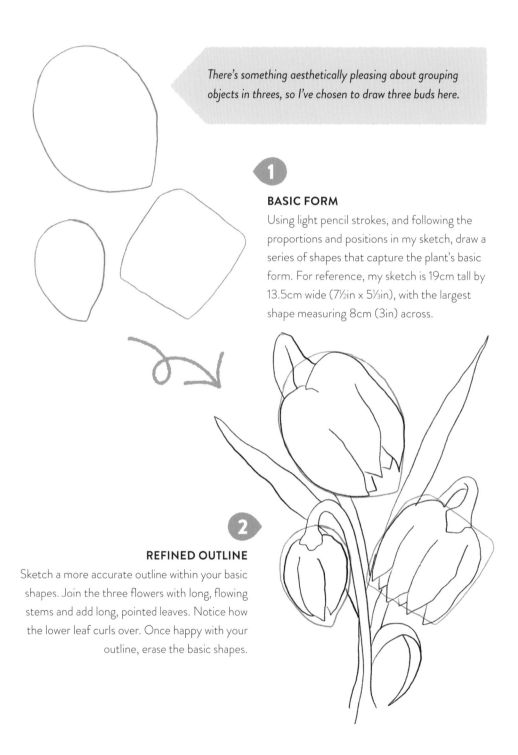

1 BASIC FORM

Using light pencil strokes, and following the proportions and positions in my sketch, draw a series of shapes that capture the plant's basic form. For reference, my sketch is 19cm tall by 13.5cm wide (7½in x 5⅓in), with the largest shape measuring 8cm (3in) across.

2 REFINED OUTLINE

Sketch a more accurate outline within your basic shapes. Join the three flowers with long, flowing stems and add long, pointed leaves. Notice how the lower leaf curls over. Once happy with your outline, erase the basic shapes.

3

PENCIL DETAILS

Using the final image as a reference, add more detail. Refine the lines of the leaves and flowers and draw in the folds of the petals. Go over the lines once more, pressing hard to create an indent to use as a border for the paint.

4

PENCIL IMPRESSION

Erase the pencil lines, leaving just the indent. If you prefer to keep a few marks, make sure you are happy for them to show through the paint.

5

FIRST FLOWER WASH

Mix permanent rose with lots of water and paint a thin wash over the three flower heads.

Brush 2
Permanent Rose

6
FIRST LEAF AND STEM WASH

Mix permanent sap green with lots of water and paint this over the leaves and stem in a smooth, flowing layer.

Brush 1
Permanent Sap Green

Brush 0
Permanent Rose
and Winsor Violet

7
SECOND FLOWER WASH

Mix permanent rose with a little Winsor violet. Starting at the top of each flower, paint thin, watery layers reaching down towards the tips of the petals. While the paint is still wet, paint more concentrated layers where the flowers meet their stems. Trace the indent lines.

8
SECOND LEAF AND STEM WASH

Mix burnt sienna and permanent sap green and paint a watery layer over just the left side of the bent stems, leaving some of the first wash visible on the right. Paint olive green over the right side of the leaves and trace the indent down the centre of each leaf.

Brush 0
Burnt Sienna and
Permanent Sap Green

Brush 0
Olive Green

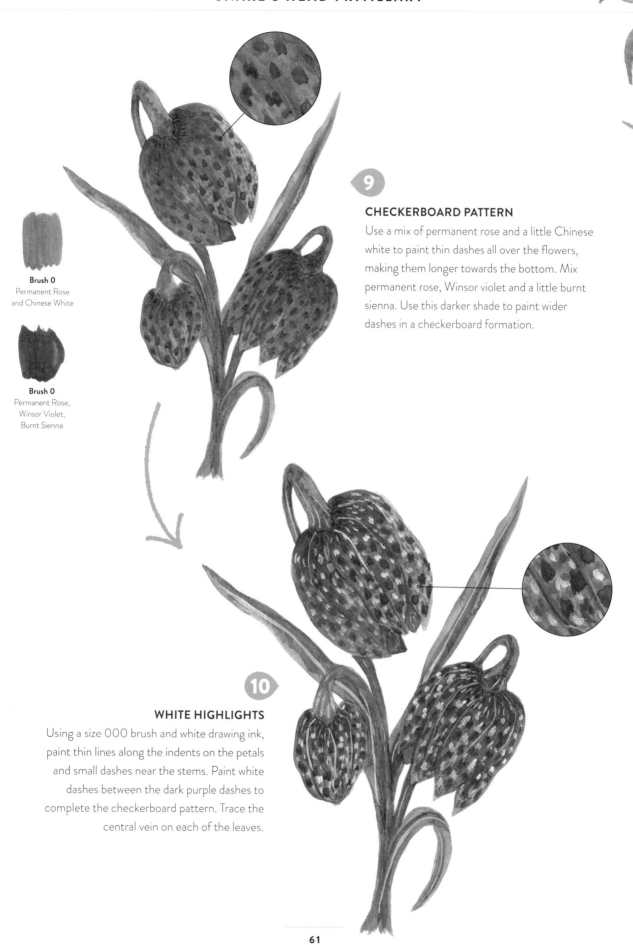

Brush 0
Permanent Rose
and Chinese White

Brush 0
Permanent Rose,
Winsor Violet,
Burnt Sienna

9 CHECKERBOARD PATTERN

Use a mix of permanent rose and a little Chinese white to paint thin dashes all over the flowers, making them longer towards the bottom. Mix permanent rose, Winsor violet and a little burnt sienna. Use this darker shade to paint wider dashes in a checkerboard formation.

10 WHITE HIGHLIGHTS

Using a size 000 brush and white drawing ink, paint thin lines along the indents on the petals and small dashes near the stems. Paint white dashes between the dark purple dashes to complete the checkerboard pattern. Trace the central vein on each of the leaves.

FORGET-ME-NOT

Myosotis arvensis

With its tiny, pale blue flowers with bright yellow centres, the forget-me-not is a cheery sight in gardens, fields and woodlands throughout the summer months.

1 BASIC FORM

Using light pencil strokes, and following the proportions and positions in my sketch, draw a series of shapes that capture the plant's basic form. For reference, my sketch is 20cm tall by 14cm wide (7¾in x 5½in), with the largest circle measuring 5cm (2in) across.

2 REFINED OUTLINE

Sketch a more accurate outline within your basic shapes. Draw clusters of five-petalled flowers within each of the circles. Notice how the leaves are quite loose, with long, pointed tips. Draw a series of stems and stalks to join the different elements together. Once happy with your outline, erase the basic shapes.

3

PENCIL DETAILS

Using the final image as a reference, add more detail. Draw some small buds coming off the flower bunches and add a central vein to each of the leaves. Go over the lines once more, pressing hard to create an indent to use as a border for the paint.

4

PENCIL IMPRESSION

Erase the pencil lines, leaving just the indent. If you prefer to keep a few marks, make sure you are happy for them to show through the paint.

Painting alternate petals in two different shades ensures a more natural-looking flower. The colours will blend where they overlap, creating more tone.

5

FIRST WASH

Mix Prussian blue and Chinese white with plenty of water and paint alternate petals and buds. Once they have dried, add a little more Prussian blue to the mix and paint the remaining petals and buds.

Brush 1
Prussian Blue and
Chinese White

6

FLOWER CENTRES

Mix a concentrated yellow ochre and aureolin to paint the centre of each flower. This should be a fairly opaque layer.

Brush 0
Yellow Ochre and
Aureolin

7

BUILDING COLOUR

Add a couple of drops of French ultramarine to the Step 5 mix, to create a brighter blue. Paint a series of dashes radiating out from the yellow centre of each flower. Add a few lines where each bud meets its stalk.

Brush 0
Prussian Blue, Chinese White,
French Ultramarine

8

FIRST LEAF AND STEM WASH

Paint the leaves with a watery mix of permanent sap green and yellow ochre. Add a drop more yellow ochre to create a slightly darker shade for the main stem. Switch to the size 1 brush to paint this darker colour on the thinner parts of the stem.

Brush 2 & 1
Permanent Sap Green
and Yellow Ochre

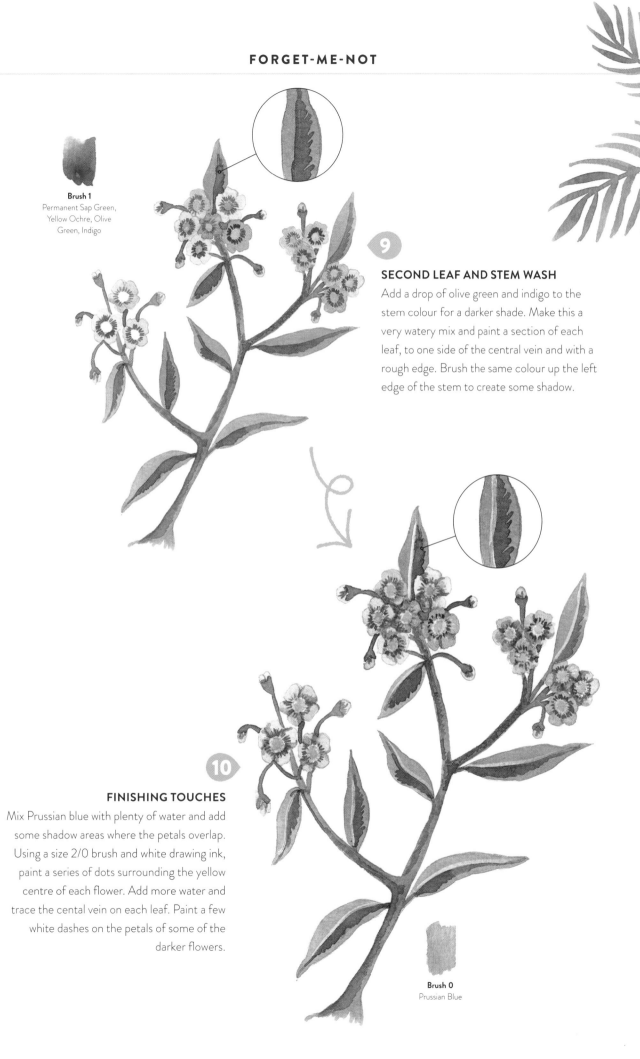

Brush 1
Permanent Sap Green,
Yellow Ochre, Olive
Green, Indigo

9

SECOND LEAF AND STEM WASH
Add a drop of olive green and indigo to the stem colour for a darker shade. Make this a very watery mix and paint a section of each leaf, to one side of the central vein and with a rough edge. Brush the same colour up the left edge of the stem to create some shadow.

10

FINISHING TOUCHES
Mix Prussian blue with plenty of water and add some shadow areas where the petals overlap. Using a size 2/0 brush and white drawing ink, paint a series of dots surrounding the yellow centre of each flower. Add more water and trace the cental vein on each leaf. Paint a few white dashes on the petals of some of the darker flowers.

Brush 0
Prussian Blue

WINTER ACONITE

Eranthis hyemalis

Winter aconite is one of the first plants to bloom in spring, lighting up the garden with its pretty, yellow, buttercup-like flowers.

1

BASIC FORM

Using light pencil strokes, and following the proportions and positions in my sketch, draw a series of shapes that capture the plant's basic form. For reference, my sketch is 20cm tall by 12cm wide (7¾in x 4¾in), with the large, horizontal oval measuring 11cm (4⅓in) across.

2

REFINED OUTLINE

Sketch a more accurate outline within your basic shapes. Note how the thin, pointed leaves radiate out from the base, and that the centre of each flower is an irregular shape surrounded by five pointed petals. Draw in the thin stem. Once happy with your outline, erase the basic shapes.

PENCIL DETAILS

Using the final image as a reference, add more detail. Refine the shapes a little and draw some line detail within the petals. Add the central vein on each leaf. Go over the lines once more, pressing hard to create an indent to use as a border for the paint.

PENCIL IMPRESSION

Erase the pencil lines, leaving just the indent. If you prefer to keep a few marks, make sure you are happy for them to show through the paint.

Brush 2
Aureolin and
Yellow Ochre

FIRST WASH

Mix aureolin and yellow ochre to paint a watery wash over the petals. Add more pigment to the brush for the central section of the top flower and the upturned petal of the central flower.

6

FLOWER CENTRES

Mix a watery yellow ochre, raw sienna and raw umber for the flower centres. Dab with a paper towel if the colour looks too dark.

Brush 2
Yellow Ochre, Raw
Sienna, Raw Umber

Brush 2
Chinese White and
Lemon Yellow

Brush 0
Yellow Ochre, Raw Sienna,
Raw Umber

7

BUILDING COLOUR

Mix Chinese white with a little lemon yellow and plenty of water. Trace the indent lines on the petals. Once dry, use the Step 6 mix to paint over the indents with thin, watery lines.

Your leaf colour should be semi-opaque so that the indents remain visible.

8

FIRST LEAF WASH

Mix permanent sap green, yellow ochre and a drop of indigo with plenty of water and paint the leaves. Switch to the size 0 brush and paint a series of small curves over the brown centre of each flower. These should be fairly haphazard in arrangement.

Brush 1 & 0
Permanent Sap Green,
Yellow Ochre, Indigo

9 LEAF DETAILS AND STEM

Mix olive green with a drop of raw umber to paint the stem. Mix sap green with indigo and plenty of water to make a darker shade of the leaf green. Starting at the base of each leaf, paint watery strokes that reach halfway into the leaf. Trace the central vein with a more concentrated mix.

Brush 1
Olive Green and Raw Umber

Brush 1
Sap Green and Indigo

10 FINISHING TOUCHES

Using the Step 5 mix, paint some shadow areas at the centre of each flower, where the petals overlap. Using a size 2/0 brush and white drawing ink, paint a series of dots within the centre of each flower. Paint thin, watery lines between the indents on the petals, and alongside the central vein on each leaf. Add a few notches up the left edge of the stem.

Brush 1
Aureolin and Yellow Ochre

FUCHSIA

Fuchsia magellanica

Native to South America, the fuchsia is known for its pretty pendant flowers. This project focuses on red and purple blooms, although they also appear in pink and lavender.

1

BASIC FORM

Using light pencil strokes, and following the proportions and positions in my sketch, draw a series of shapes that capture the plant's basic form. For reference, my sketch is 18cm tall by 13cm wide (7in x 5in), with each diamond shape measuring around 10.5cm x 6.5cm (4in x 2½in).

2

REFINED OUTLINE

Sketch a more accurate outline within your basic shapes. Notice how the flowers hang down loosely from the stem in clusters. Draw in the outer sepals, the petals and the long stamens. Once happy with your outline, erase the basic shapes.

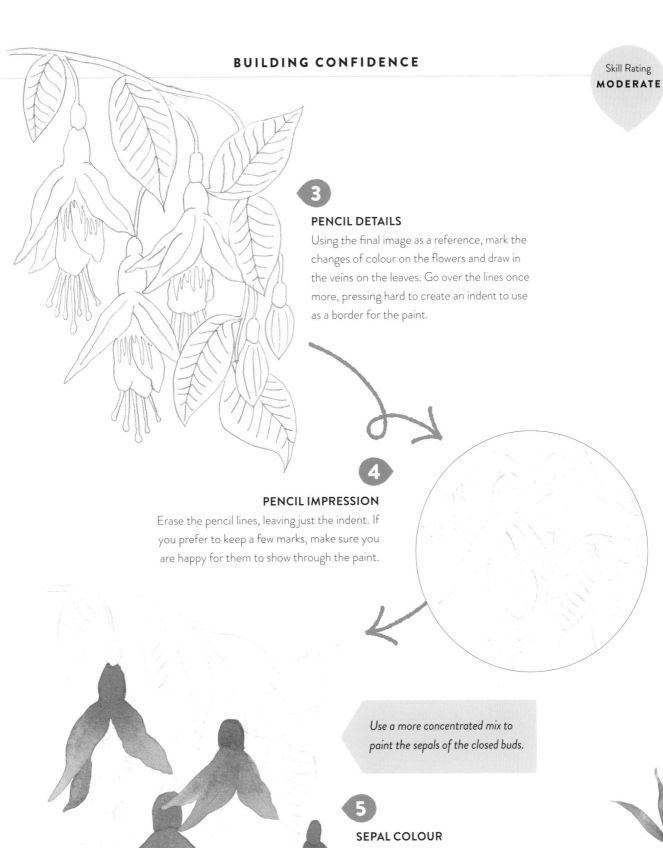

3

PENCIL DETAILS

Using the final image as a reference, mark the changes of colour on the flowers and draw in the veins on the leaves. Go over the lines once more, pressing hard to create an indent to use as a border for the paint.

4

PENCIL IMPRESSION

Erase the pencil lines, leaving just the indent. If you prefer to keep a few marks, make sure you are happy for them to show through the paint.

Use a more concentrated mix to paint the sepals of the closed buds.

5

SEPAL COLOUR

Mix permanent alizarin crimson with permanent rose and a little water. Use this to paint just the sepals of the flowers. Using more water, allow the pigment to bleed down from the stem end to the tip of each sepal.

Brush 2
Permanent Alizarin
Crimson and
Permanent Rose

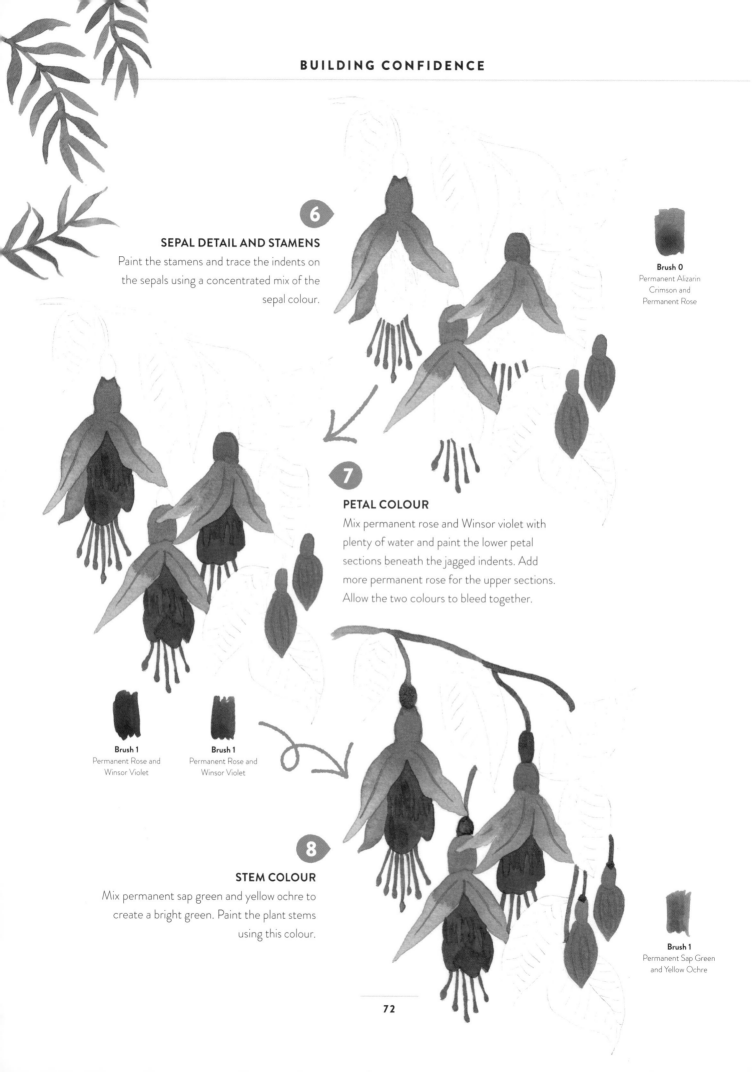

6

SEPAL DETAIL AND STAMENS

Paint the stamens and trace the indents on the sepals using a concentrated mix of the sepal colour.

Brush 0
Permanent Alizarin
Crimson and
Permanent Rose

7

PETAL COLOUR

Mix permanent rose and Winsor violet with plenty of water and paint the lower petal sections beneath the jagged indents. Add more permanent rose for the upper sections. Allow the two colours to bleed together.

Brush 1
Permanent Rose and
Winsor Violet

Brush 1
Permanent Rose and
Winsor Violet

8

STEM COLOUR

Mix permanent sap green and yellow ochre to create a bright green. Paint the plant stems using this colour.

Brush 1
Permanent Sap Green
and Yellow Ochre

9

LEAF COLOUR

Add a drop of indigo to the stem colour and paint all of the leaves with just enough water that you can see the indents showing through.

Brush 2
Permanent Sap Green,
Yellow Ochre, Indigo

10

FINISHING TOUCHES

Add more indigo to the leaf mix and paint the central vein on each leaf. Use a watery mix to paint the veins fanning out either side. Using a size 2/0 brush and white drawing ink, paint a highlight alongside each indent on the sepals. Add water and paint highlights where the buds and flowers meet the stem, on the purple petal sections and alongside the veins on the leaves. Paint a dot of white at the tip of each stamen.

Brush 0
Permanent Sap
Green, Yellow
Ochre, Indigo

TULIP

Tulipa 'Sorbet'

Tulips are one of the most iconic symbols of spring.
This variety has large, cream flowers with hot pink flushes.

1

BASIC FORM

Using light pencil strokes, and following the proportions and positions in my sketch, draw a series of shapes that capture the plant's basic form. For reference, my sketch is 18cm tall by 13cm wide (7in x 5in), with each of the ovals measuring 7cm x 4cm (2¾in x 1½in).

2

REFINED OUTLINE

Sketch a more accurate outline within your basic shapes. Note how the outer petals wrap around the inner petals, and the long, curled leaves wrap around the stems. Once happy with your outline, erase the basic shapes.

Skill Rating
MODERATE

3

PENCIL DETAILS

Using the final image as a reference, add more detail. Draw patterns on the petals, to mark changes in colour. Add a central vein to each of the leaves. Go over the lines, pressing hard to create an indent to use as a border for the paint.

4

PENCIL IMPRESSION

Erase the pencil lines, leaving just the indent. If you prefer to keep a few marks, make sure you are happy for them to show through the paint.

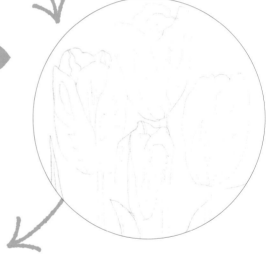

Brush 2
Lemon Yellow,
Permanent Rose,
Chinese White

Brush 2
Chinese White

Allow the outer petals to dry completely before painting the inner petals.

5

FIRST WASH

Paint the outer petals with a watery lemon yellow, permanent rose and Chinese white mix. Add more pigment to paint the inner petals in a slightly darker shade. Mix Chinese white with plenty of water and paint a layer over the flowers to soften the colours.

 6

HOT PINK FLUSHES

Add permanent rose and permanent alizarin crimson to the petal colour and paint flushes of hot pink on the petals. Keep them watery, so the paint bleeds into the pale layers below.

Brush 1
Lemon Yellow,
Permanent Rose,
Chinese White,
Permanent Alizarin
Crimson

Brush 2
Lemon Yellow, Permanent
Rose, Chinese White,
Permanent Alizarin
Crimson, Winsor Red

 7

BUILDING COLOUR

Add Winsor red to the hot pink and use a concentrated mix over the darker petal areas, leaving obvious brushstrokes at the edges. Add lots of water and paint a watery layer were the petals join the stem.

8

LEAF COLOUR

Mix permanent sap green with plenty of water and paint the leaves in the foreground. Add more pigment to create a darker shade for the leaves in the background. Use the same shade to paint the central vein on each leaf.

Brush 2
Permanent Sap Green

Brush 1 & 0
Permanent Sap Green
and Yellow Ochre

9

LEAF DETAIL

Add yellow ochre and enough water to the
leaf colour to make it a semi-opaque mix.
Paint the flower stems. Switch to the size
0 brush and paint thin, watery ribbon
strokes up each leaf. Follow the natural
curves and vary the amount of pigment
to achieve a range of light and dark tones.

*If the tulips have too much white on
them, just add more water to the Step
7 mix and apply this over the top.*

10

WHITE HIGHLIGHTS

Using a size 1 brush and white drawing ink,
paint thick white streaks over the pale pink of
the tulip petals. Working dry-on-dry, blend
the white ink into the red slightly. Add lots of
water to a size 0 brush and trace some of the
contours on the leaves.

SWEET PEA

Lathyrus odoratus

This climbing plant flowers in late summer and autumn, its vinelike stems
awash with fragrant flowers in white, pink, red, violet and purple.

1

BASIC FORM

Using light pencil strokes, and following the
proportions and positions in my sketch, draw a
series of shapes that capture the plant's basic
form. For reference, my sketch is 17cm tall
by 13cm wide (6⅔in x 5in), with each flower
shape around 4cm (1½in) across.

*To add variety here, make the flowers different
sizes and with a range of shapes for their petals.*

2

REFINED OUTLINE

Sketch a more accurate outline within your
basic shapes. Each flower has just two or three
petals. Flesh out the stems and draw in some
thin, pointed leaves. Once happy with your
outline, erase the basic shapes.

PENCIL DETAILS

Using the final image as a reference, refine the shapes of the petals and add long, thin tendrils coming off the stalks. Draw in the central vein of each leaf. Go over the lines once more, pressing hard to create an indent to use as a border for the paint.

PENCIL IMPRESSION

Erase the pencil lines, leaving just the indent. If you prefer to keep a few marks, make sure you are happy for them to show through the paint.

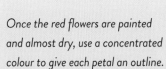

Once the red flowers are painted and almost dry, use a concentrated colour to give each petal an outline.

Brush 2
Permanent Rose, Winsor
Red, Winsor Orange

FIRST COLOUR WASH

Mix permanent rose, Winsor red and Winsor orange with plenty of water. To paint each red flower, wash water over the outer petals. Drop some paint where the outer petals meet and watch the colour bleed. Dab the petals here and there to create a faded look.

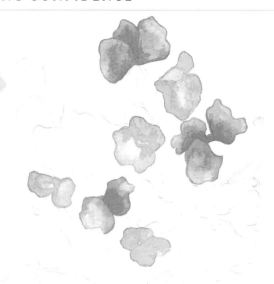

When mixed together, pink and yellow often separate on the page, but this lends itself well to sweet pea petals.

Brush 2
Lemon Yellow and
Permanent Rose

6

SECOND COLOUR WASH

Mix lemon yellow and permanent rose with lots of water to create a pale, peachy colour. Paint three or four of the smaller flowers using the same technique as for Step 5.

Brush 2
Cerulean Blue and
Winsor Violet

7

THIRD COLOUR WASH

Mix cerulean blue with a drop of Winsor violet and lots of water. Paint the remaining flowers using the same technique as for Step 5.

8

LEAF AND STEM COLOUR

Mix a light green for the leaves and stems using permanent sap green and lemon yellow. Keep the mix quite watery. Once the first wash is dry, add a little more pigment at the base of each leaf, blending slightly up the leaf.

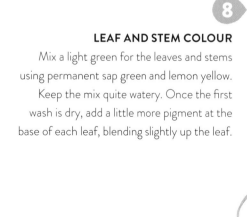

Brush 0
Permanent Sap Green
and Lemon Yellow

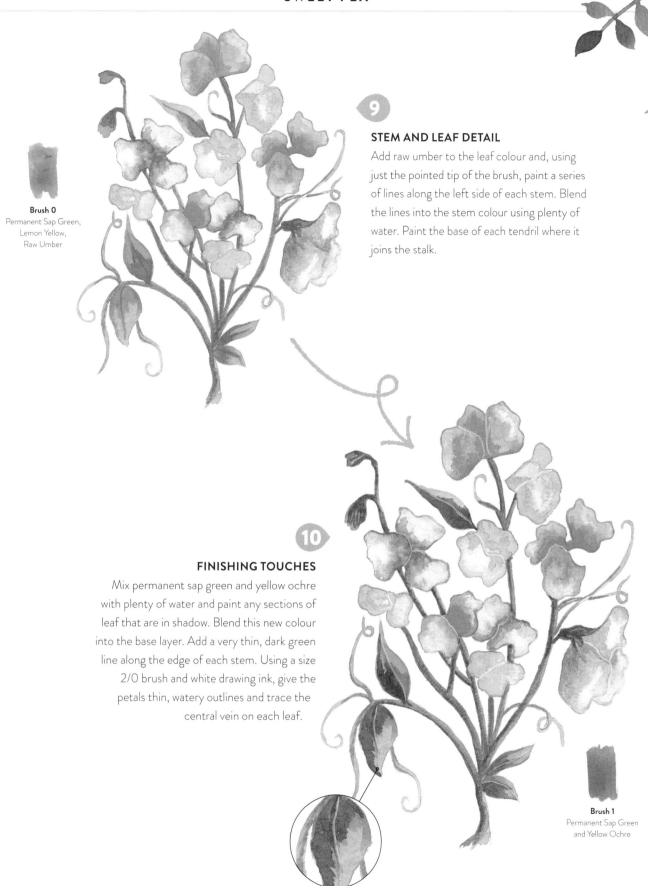

Brush 0
Permanent Sap Green,
Lemon Yellow,
Raw Umber

9

STEM AND LEAF DETAIL

Add raw umber to the leaf colour and, using just the pointed tip of the brush, paint a series of lines along the left side of each stem. Blend the lines into the stem colour using plenty of water. Paint the base of each tendril where it joins the stalk.

10

FINISHING TOUCHES

Mix permanent sap green and yellow ochre with plenty of water and paint any sections of leaf that are in shadow. Blend this new colour into the base layer. Add a very thin, dark green line along the edge of each stem. Using a size 2/0 brush and white drawing ink, give the petals thin, watery outlines and trace the central vein on each leaf.

Brush 1
Permanent Sap Green
and Yellow Ochre

PEONY

Paeonia

The many different varieties of peony grow in a wide range of colours.
Common to all of them are their multi-petalled flower heads.

1

BASIC FORM

Using light pencil strokes, and following the
proportions and positions in my sketch, draw a
series of shapes that capture the bloom's basic
form. For reference, my sketch is 18cm tall by
13cm wide (7in x 5in), with the central circle
around 13cm (5in) across.

2

REFINED OUTLINE

Sketch a more accurate outline within your
basic shapes. Clustered tightly, the petals are
larger at the bottom of the flower, decreasing
in size towards the centre. Note that they
have fairly crinkled edges. Draw the shapely
leaves. Once happy with your outline, erase
the basic shapes.

PENCIL DETAILS

Using the final image as a reference, draw a cluster of small circles at the centre of the flower and some lines rising up the petals. Give the leaves some veins. Go over the lines once more, pressing hard to create an indent to use as a border for the paint.

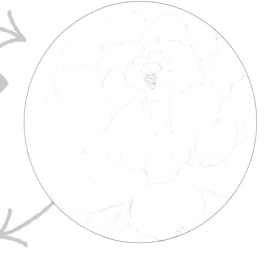

PENCIL IMPRESSION

Erase the pencil lines, leaving just the indent. If you prefer to keep a few marks, make sure you are happy for them to show through the paint.

Work outwards from the centre of the flower, painting each petal in turn to retain the separate petal structure.

BASE COLOUR

Create a soft apricot colour using Chinese white, lemon yellow and a drop of Winsor red. Paint a watery wash over each of the petals, varying the pigment ratios to achieve a range of tones. Paint a more concentrated mix at the base of each petal and use lots of water to blend the colour upwards.

Brush 2
Chinese White, Lemon
Yellow, Winsor Red

When working through Steps 6 and 7, if any of your colours look too dark, simply dab them with a paper towel and apply a water wash over the top.

 6

TONE AND TEXTURE

Mix Chinese white and Winsor red with plenty of water. Paint watery pink streaks rising from the base of each petal to about halfway up. Follow the indents and the curves of the petals. Use the same pink to fill in areas of shade where petals are folded over.

Brush 2
Chinese White and
Winsor Red

Brush 2
Permanent Rose
and Lemon Yellow

 7

CREATING DEPTH

Mix permanent rose and lemon yellow with plenty of water. Repeat step 6, adding this darker shade at the base of the petals in the foreground to create more depth. Paint a watery wash of this colour over any petals that look too yellow. Give each petal a very thin, watery outline.

 8

BUILDING COLOUR

Mix a concentrated yellow ochre to paint the centre of the flower, leaving the paper showing through here and there. Mix permanent sap green and yellow ochre for the base leaf colour. Once almost dry, add more pigment to the mix and trace the central vein on each leaf.

Brush 0
Yellow Ochre

Brush 2
Permanent Sap Green
and Yellow Ochre

Brush 2
Permanent Sap Green,
Yellow Ochre, Indigo

9
LEAF DETAIL

Add more permanent sap green and a drop of indigo to the base leaf colour. Using a little water, paint over the indents on the leaves, and blend the colour out towards the edges using plenty of water. Apply more pigment where the leaves are in shadow.

10
WHITE HIGHLIGHTS

Using a size 2/0 brush and white drawing ink, paint thin highlights over the petals, softening any layers that look too dark. Trace the veins on the leaves. Remember to dab the paint with a paper towel if you apply too much.

CAMELLIA

Camellia japonica

Sometimes called a winter rose, the camellia is an early flowering shrub with dark green glossy leaves. The petals of its showy flowers run in concentric circles.

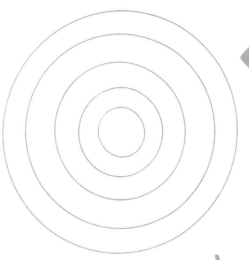

1 BASIC FORM

Working lightly with a pencil, draw a circle roughly 9cm (3½in) in diameter. Use a compass if you'd like to be neat. Draw four inner circles at roughly even intervals, with the smallest around 1.5cm (⅔in) in diameter.

2 REFINED OUTLINE

Draw a series of petals within the circular guides. Start at the centre and work your way out. Notice how the petals are tightly wound at the centre, getting larger and looser as they radiate out, with the larger petals having pointed tips. Once happy with your outline, erase the basic shapes.

3

PENCIL DETAILS

Using the final image as a reference, refine the shapes of the petals and draw in a sprig of leaves. As a guide, my sketch is 16cm tall by 14cm wide (6⅓in x 5⅔in). Go over the lines once more, pressing hard to create an indent to use as a border for the paint.

4

PENCIL IMPRESSION

Erase the pencil lines, leaving just the indent. If you prefer to keep a few marks, make sure you are happy for them to show through the paint.

5

FIRST WASH

Mix Chinese white, Winsor red and plenty of water. Apply a really watery wash over all the petals in a sweep.

Brush 2
Chinese White
and Winsor Red

6

INNER PETALS

Using concentrated mixes, paint the inner rounds of petals in the following colours, working out from the centre: permanent alizarin crimson; permanent rose; and the Step 5 mix. Paint each petal separately and allow it to dry before painting the next. When the paint is dry, use the Step 5 mix to paint a watery outline around each round of petals.

Brush 0
Permanent Rose

Brush 0
Permanent Alizarin Crimson

Brush 0
Chinese White and Winsor Red

Brush 0
Chinese White and Winsor Red

7

OUTER PETALS

Work in the same way to paint the outer rounds of petals, using the Step 5 mix and much more water with each subsequent round. Add a few lines rising up from the base of each outer petal, allowing them to fade gradually.

8

LEAF BASE COLOUR

Mix olive green, indigo and yellow ochre to create a browny green. Using plenty of water, paint this over the leaves. This should be just a wash. Use the size 0 brush to paint the same colour over the stem.

Brush 2 & 0
Olive Green, Indigo, Yellow Ochre

Brush 2
Permanent Sap Green,
Yellow Ochre, Indigo

9

LEAF TONE AND TEXTURE

Add some permanent sap green and plenty of water to the leaf base colour, and apply a layer where the leaves are in shadow. Dab lightly with the brush to blend the colour in. Paint a thin line over the right side of the stem, allowing the colours to bend slightly.

10

WHITE HIGHLIGHTS

Using a size 0 brush and white drawing ink, paint watery highlights at the outermost edges of the petals and trace the central vein of each glossy leaf. Using a size 2/0 brush, draw a thin outline around the central cluster of petals.

3

MASTERING THE ART

The projects in this section have intricate pencil drawings and much of the hard work is done in these early steps. Here comes the chance to really finesse your colour mixing for the passionflower and to hone your fine-painting skills for the patterning on the zebra plant and slipper orchid. Turn to the hydrangea and monstera projects to practise working wet-on-wet.

CORNFLOWER

Centaurea cyanus

Cornflowers got their name because they used to grow as weeds in cornfields. These wildflowers are also known as bachelor's buttons and blue bonnets.

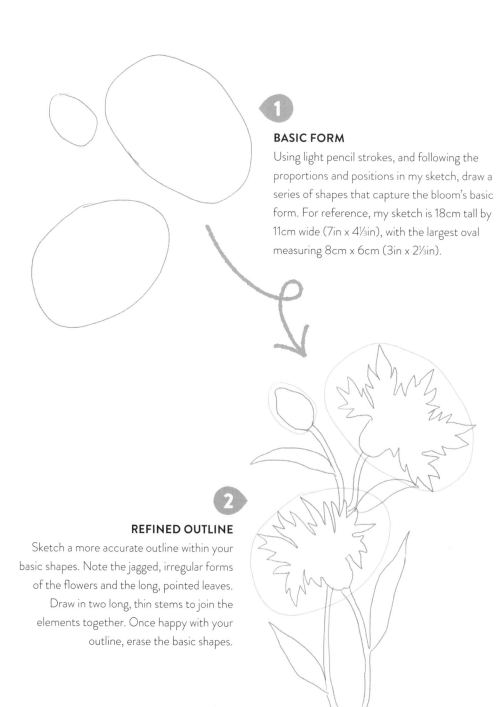

1

BASIC FORM
Using light pencil strokes, and following the proportions and positions in my sketch, draw a series of shapes that capture the bloom's basic form. For reference, my sketch is 18cm tall by 11cm wide (7in x 4⅓in), with the largest oval measuring 8cm x 6cm (3in x 2⅓in).

2

REFINED OUTLINE
Sketch a more accurate outline within your basic shapes. Note the jagged, irregular forms of the flowers and the long, pointed leaves. Draw in two long, thin stems to join the elements together. Once happy with your outline, erase the basic shapes.

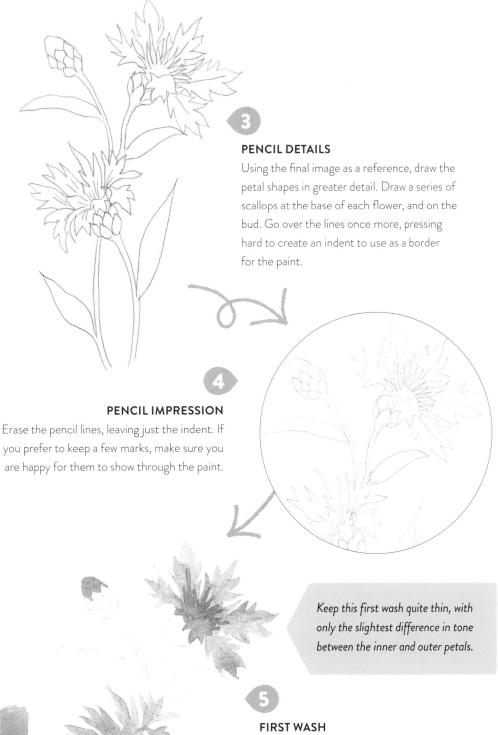

3 PENCIL DETAILS

Using the final image as a reference, draw the petal shapes in greater detail. Draw a series of scallops at the base of each flower, and on the bud. Go over the lines once more, pressing hard to create an indent to use as a border for the paint.

4 PENCIL IMPRESSION

Erase the pencil lines, leaving just the indent. If you prefer to keep a few marks, make sure you are happy for them to show through the paint.

Keep this first wash quite thin, with only the slightest difference in tone between the inner and outer petals.

5 FIRST WASH

Mix Prussian blue with lots of water and paint a wash over the outer petals of both flowers and the top of the bud. Add more pigment to your brush for the inner petals.

Brush 1
Prussian Blue

6

SECOND WASH

Mix cerulean blue, Prussian blue and Winsor blue with plenty of water. Paint thin lines from the base of each flower towards the tips of the petals. Paint the lower half of the bud.

Brush 1
Cerulean Blue, Prussian Blue, Winsor Blue

Brush 0
Prussian Blue, Winsor Purple, Cerulean Blue, Chinese White

7

THIRD WASH

Mix Prussian blue, Winsor purple, cerulean blue and Chinese white to paint more lines from the base of the petals to the tips, and a small amount at the bottom of the bud. Use water to blend the paint with the layers below. Use a very watery mix to give the petals a very fine outline.

Blending this new colour with the layers below will create subtle variations that give the flower a more natural, organic look.

8

LEAF AND STEM COLOUR

Mix olive green and lemon yellow with plenty of water. Apply a wash over the leaves, stems and bud. Make sure you can see the indents through the paint. When the paint has dried a little, paint a watery brushstroke over the middle of each leaf.

Brush 1
Olive Green and Lemon Yellow

Brush 1
Olive Green, Lemon Yellow,
Permanent Sap Green

Brush 2/0
Olive Green, Lemon Yellow,
Permanent Sap Green,
Burnt Umber

9

LEAF AND STEM DETAIL

Add permanent sap green and plenty of water
to the leaf colour. Paint thick brushstrokes
up the leaves. Use the tip of the brush to
paint horizontal lines down the right side of
the stem. Add more water and paint inside
the scallop segments. Add burnt umber and
slightly less water to give the scallops an
outline. Paint thin, watery lines where the
leaves join the stems and along the right edges
of the stems.

10

WHITE HIGHLIGHTS

Using white drawing ink and a size 2/0
brush, paint watery highlights on the left side
of the bud, blending them into the blue. Paint
a series of thin, white lines over the darkest
areas of the petals. Using lots of water, draw a
couple of highlights along the left side of the
stem sections and on some of the leaves.

ZEBRA PLANT

Haworthia fasciata

Native to South Africa, this spiky succulent has distinctive green,
fleshy leaves, etched with white stripes.

1 BASIC FORM

Using light pencil strokes, draw a large
teardrop shape for the basic shape of
your plant. For reference, mine measured
14cm x 9cm (5½in x 3½in).

2 REFINED OUTLINE

Sketch a more accurate outline within your
basic shape, drawing long, pointed leaves that
reach up the page. Draw lots of layers, with
a few thinner leaves poking up, away from
the guidelines. Once happy with your outline,
erase the basic shapes.

 3

PENCIL DETAILS

Using the final image as a reference, refine the edges of the leaves – they should be quite bumpy. Add the 'zebra' stripes all the way up the leaves. Go over the lines once more, pressing hard to create an indent to use as a border for the paint.

 4

PENCIL IMPRESSION

Erase the pencil lines, leaving just the indent. If you prefer to keep a few marks, make sure you are happy for them to show through the paint.

You need to be quite neat here. Start at either the top or the bottom of a leaf, to stop you getting confused as to which stripe should be green or white.

Brush 0
Permanent Sap Green
and Olive Green

 5

FIRST WASH

Mix permanent sap green and olive green with plenty of water. Carefully paint each leaf, one at a time, and with varying amounts of pigment to vary the tone.

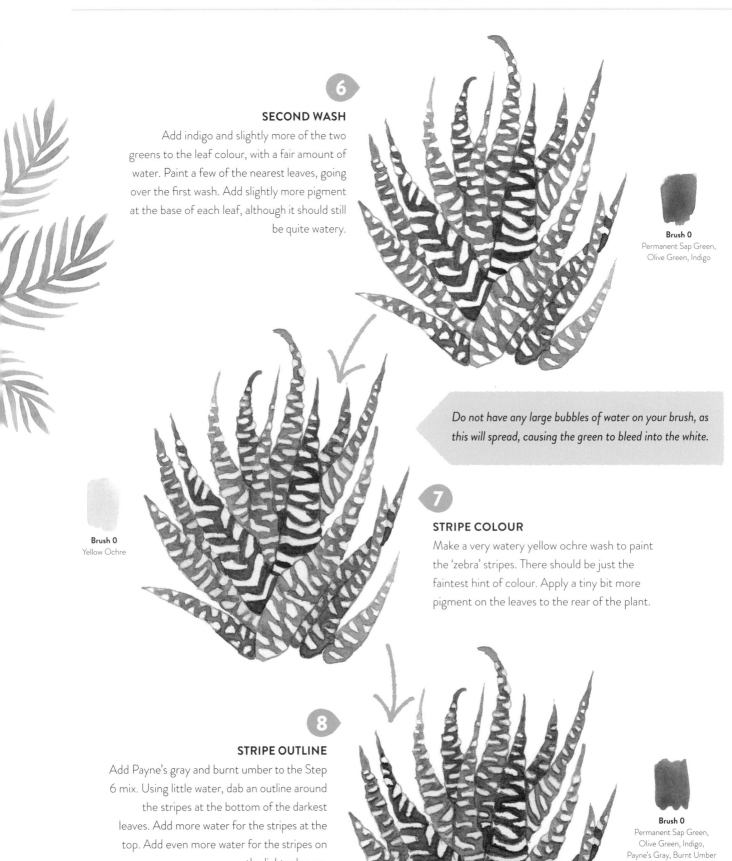

6
SECOND WASH

Add indigo and slightly more of the two greens to the leaf colour, with a fair amount of water. Paint a few of the nearest leaves, going over the first wash. Add slightly more pigment at the base of each leaf, although it should still be quite watery.

Brush 0
Permanent Sap Green, Olive Green, Indigo

Do not have any large bubbles of water on your brush, as this will spread, causing the green to bleed into the white.

Brush 0
Yellow Ochre

7
STRIPE COLOUR

Make a very watery yellow ochre wash to paint the 'zebra' stripes. There should be just the faintest hint of colour. Apply a tiny bit more pigment on the leaves to the rear of the plant.

8
STRIPE OUTLINE

Add Payne's gray and burnt umber to the Step 6 mix. Using little water, dab an outline around the stripes at the bottom of the darkest leaves. Add more water for the stripes at the top. Add even more water for the stripes on the lighter leaves.

Brush 0
Permanent Sap Green, Olive Green, Indigo, Payne's Gray, Burnt Umber

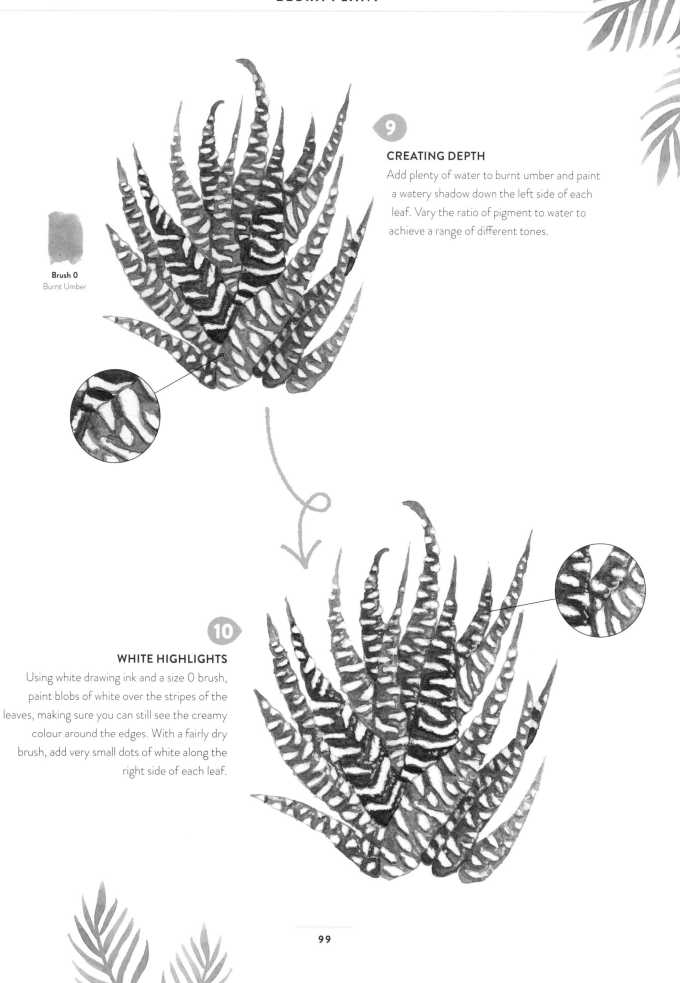

Brush 0
Burnt Umber

9

CREATING DEPTH
Add plenty of water to burnt umber and paint a watery shadow down the left side of each leaf. Vary the ratio of pigment to water to achieve a range of different tones.

10

WHITE HIGHLIGHTS
Using white drawing ink and a size 0 brush, paint blobs of white over the stripes of the leaves, making sure you can still see the creamy colour around the edges. With a fairly dry brush, add very small dots of white along the right side of each leaf.

HYDRANGEA

Hydrangea macrophylla

Hydrangeas are some of the most recognizable garden shrubs, their soft, cloudlike blooms seen in many a garden throughout the summer.

1

BASIC FORM

Using light pencil strokes, and following the proportions and positions in my sketch, draw a series of shapes that capture the plant's basic form. For reference, my sketch is 20cm tall by 14cm wide (8in x 5½in), with the largest circle around 10cm (4in) across.

2

REFINED OUTLINE

Sketch a more accurate outline within your basic shape. Hydrangea blooms have many clusters of petals, so make the edges of each flower rough and bumpy. Draw some leaf shapes within the ovals, and draw in their veins. Once happy with your outline, erase the basic shapes.

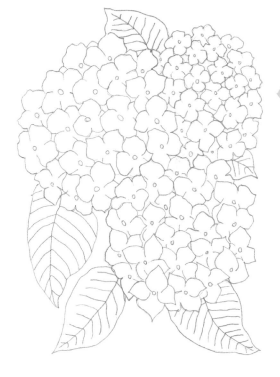

 3

PENCIL DETAILS

Using the final image as a reference, populate each flower shape with petal clusters. Make the petals on the rear flower smaller, to help gain a sense of perspective. Go over the lines once more, pressing hard to create an indent to use as a border for the paint.

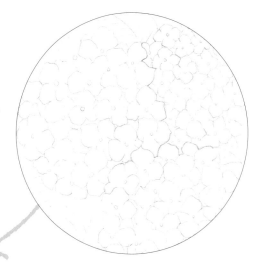

 4

PENCIL IMPRESSION

Erase the pencil lines, leaving just the indent. If you prefer to keep a few marks, make sure you are happy for them to show through the paint.

Take care around the outer edges so that you retain the flower shape and it looks neat.

Brush 2
Prussian Blue and
Permanent Rose

 5

FIRST WASH

Mix Prussian blue and permanent rose with lots of water. Paint a thin, watery wash over the flowers, varying the ratio of pigment to water to create a range of hues and tones. Take care to maintain clear definition between the three flowers.

BUILDING COLOUR

Add cerulean blue to the first wash. Paint a watery line around each petal and work the colour in, stopping short of the centre. Vary the pigment/water ratio as before. Use a concentrated mix to paint shadow areas between the petals.

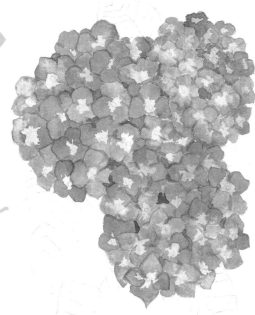

Brush 1
Prussian Blue,
Permanent Rose,
Cerulean Blue

FINE DETAIL

Mix Prussian blue with plenty of water. Paint a dot at the centre of each petal group and draw faint, curved lines radiating out from it. Add more water and paint a watery blue outline around the two front flowers where they meet the smallest one at the back.

Brush 2/0
Prussian Blue

LEAF COLOUR

Mix yellow ochre and permanent sap green with plenty of water. Paint over the leaves, making sure you can still see the indents. Use more pigment on the right side of each leaf and allow the colour to bleed into the left side.

Brush 2
Yellow Ochre and
Permanent Sap Green

Brush 1
Yellow Ochre,
Permanent Sap
Green, Indigo

Brush 0
Burnt Umber

Brush 0
Yellow Ochre,
Permanent Sap Green,
Indigo, Burnt Umber

9 LEAF DETAIL

Mix indigo into the leaf colour. Using plenty of water, paint between the veins on each leaf. Work from the centre outwards, blending the colour into the lighter green. Make a watery burnt umber mix. Once the green layer is almost dry, paint over the veins. Mix a little burnt umber into the green mix. Using lots of water, draw the brush along the right edge of each leaf to create shadow.

Brush 0
Payne's Gray and
Cerulean Blue

10 FINISHING TOUCHES

Mix a watery Payne's gray and cerulean blue to paint shadow areas on and around the petals to the right of the painting. Use a watery white drawing ink and a size 2/0 brush to paint highlights on the petals to the left. Draw a more concentrated white line around each central dot, and along the central vein on each leaf. Paint a few watery lines on the left side of each leaf and blend them in.

SLIPPER ORCHID

Paphiopedilum

For this project, you will use the wet-on-wet method to paint the slipper-like pouch from which the orchid takes its name.

1

BASIC FORM

Using light pencil strokes, and following the proportions and positions in my sketch, draw a series of shapes that capture the orchid's basic form. For reference, my sketch is 17cm tall by 12cm wide (6⅔in x 4¾in), with the large teardrop shape measuring 14cm x 11cm (5½in x 4⅓in).

2

REFINED OUTLINE

Sketch a more accurate outline within your basic shapes. The flower is quite simple in construction, with a sepal at the top, the pouch below and a petal to either side. Draw in the stem and leaves. Once happy with your outline, erase the basic shapes.

PENCIL DETAILS

Using the final image as a reference, draw in the distinctive patterning on the sepal and petals. Add more detail and shape to the central section of the flower. Draw sweeping lines up both leaves. Go over the lines once more, pressing hard to create an indent to use as a border for the paint.

PENCIL IMPRESSION

Erase the pencil lines, leaving just the indent. If you prefer to keep a few marks, make sure you are happy for them to show through the paint.

Brush 2
Lemon Yellow, Olive Green,
Permanent Sap Green

Dab the lower sections of the petals with a paper towel to make them much lighter in colour.

FIRST WASH

Mix lemon yellow, olive green and permanent sap green. Using lots of water, paint the petals and sepal from the centre outwards so that the colour gradually fades. Allow this layer to dry before painting a more concentrated colour at the centre of the flower, adding more sap green to the mix.

6

SECOND WASH

Paint the top of the sepal and lower central section with a very watery lemon yellow and yellow ochre mix. When this has dried, paint the very centre with a concentrated yellow ochre. Mix a fluid permanent rose to trace the indents on the sepal. Add lots more water and trace the indents at the tips of the petals.

Brush 2
Lemon Yellow and Yellow Ochre

Brush 2
Yellow Ochre

Brush 0
Permanent Rose

Brush 2/0
Permanent Rose, Permanent Alizarin Crimson, Indigo, Yellow Ochre

7

BUILDING COLOUR

Mix a deep, rich, concentrated purple using permanent rose, permanent alizarin crimson, indigo and a drop of yellow ochre. Using the tip of the brush, paint very thin lines over and between the indents on the sepal. Add more water and paint a purple layer over the pale yellow lower central section.

Brush 2
Permanent Rose, Permanent Alizarin Crimson, Indigo, Yellow Ochre

Brush 1
Burnt Umber

Brush 1
Permanent Rose, Permanent Alizarin Crimson, Indigo, Yellow Ochre, Burnt Umber

8

POUCH AND STEM

Paint the pouch using the Step 7 colour, bleeding the pigment up from the base and using lots of water. Dab with a paper towel to achieve lighter patches. Work a little concentrated burnt umber into the wet purple to the right. Once dry, paint the stem and a few dots at the top of the yellow centre using burnt umber mixed with a drop of purple.

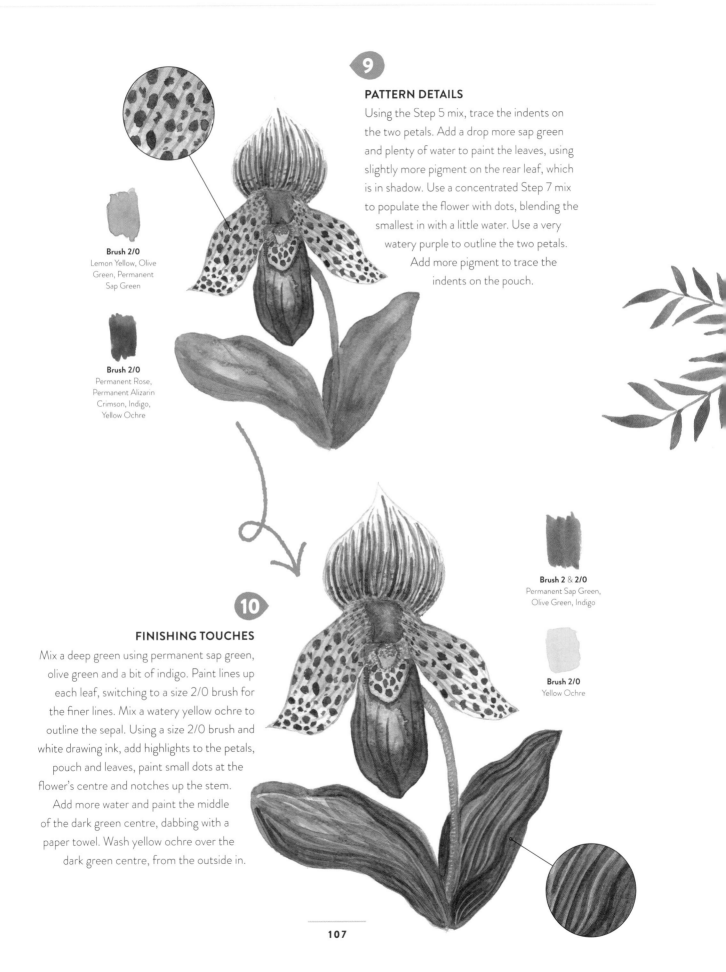

9

PATTERN DETAILS

Using the Step 5 mix, trace the indents on the two petals. Add a drop more sap green and plenty of water to paint the leaves, using slightly more pigment on the rear leaf, which is in shadow. Use a concentrated Step 7 mix to populate the flower with dots, blending the smallest in with a little water. Use a very watery purple to outline the two petals. Add more pigment to trace the indents on the pouch.

Brush 2/0
Lemon Yellow, Olive Green, Permanent Sap Green

Brush 2/0
Permanent Rose, Permanent Alizarin Crimson, Indigo, Yellow Ochre

Brush 2 & 2/0
Permanent Sap Green, Olive Green, Indigo

Brush 2/0
Yellow Ochre

10

FINISHING TOUCHES

Mix a deep green using permanent sap green, olive green and a bit of indigo. Paint lines up each leaf, switching to a size 2/0 brush for the finer lines. Mix a watery yellow ochre to outline the sepal. Using a size 2/0 brush and white drawing ink, add highlights to the petals, pouch and leaves, paint small dots at the flower's centre and notches up the stem.

Add more water and paint the middle of the dark green centre, dabbing with a paper towel. Wash yellow ochre over the dark green centre, from the outside in.

SWISS CHEESE PLANT

Monstera deliciosa 'Albo Variegata'

This Swiss cheese plant presents the challenge of rendering white. Rather than copying the painting, follow the method to achieve variegated leaves of your own.

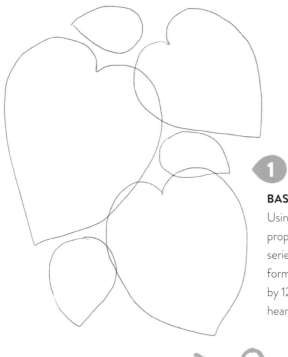

1 BASIC FORM

Using light pencil strokes, and following the proportions and positions in my sketch, draw a series of shapes that capture the plant's basic form. For reference, my sketch is 16cm tall by 12.5cm wide (6¼in x 5in), with the largest heart shape roughly 10cm x 8cm (4in x 3in).

2 REFINED OUTLINE

Sketch a more accurate outline within your basic shapes. Each leaf should be a loose heart shape that tapers to a fine point. Notice how all the stems emerge from the same spot. Draw them in and add the central vein on each leaf. Once happy with your outline, erase the basic shapes.

3

PENCIL DETAILS

Using the final image as a reference, draw in the typical cheese-plant characteristics of each leaf. Go over the lines once more, pressing hard to create an indent to use as a border for the paint.

4

PENCIL IMPRESSION

Erase the pencil lines, leaving just the indent. If you prefer to keep a few marks, make sure you are happy for them to show through the paint.

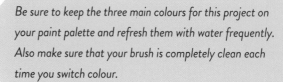

Be sure to keep the three main colours for this project on your paint palette and refresh them with water frequently. Also make sure that your brush is completely clean each time you switch colour.

Brush 1
Permanent Sap Green,
Olive Green, Indigo

5

LEAF COLOUR

Mix permanent sap green and olive green with a little indigo to make a deep, rich green. Add plenty of water and paint just the three smallest leaves.

6

FIRST VARIEGATION LAYER

Paint each of the large leaves in the following way. Mix Chinese white with a drop of lemon yellow and plenty of water, and paint one half of the leaf. With the paint still wet, dip a clean brush into the Step 5 mix. Using plenty of water, drop some of this green onto an area of cream and allow the colours to bleed together. Repeat on one or two other areas of the cream layer.

Brush 2
Chinese White and
Lemon Yellow

Brush 2
Permanent Sap Green,
Olive Green, Indigo

Brush 2
Permanent Sap Green,
Olive Green, Indigo,
Burnt Umber

Brush 2
Permanent Sap Green,
Olive Green, Indigo

7

SECOND VARIEGATION LAYER

Repeat Step 6 to paint the opposite side of the largest leaves. This time, start with a deep, inky mix of permanent sap green, olive green, indigo and burnt umber. Then, blend in a little of the Step 5 green. Leave some areas of the leaves unpainted also.

Brush 2
Permanent Sap Green,
Olive Green, Indigo

Brush 2
Permanent Sap Green,
Olive Green, Indigo,
Burnt Umber

8

THIRD VARIEGATION LAYER

Work on each large leaf in turn. Add lots of water to your brush and dip it into the Step 5 mix. Paint a watery layer over any blank area, dabbing with a paper towel if it is too wet or dark. Work wet-on-wet to add cream or dark green to some areas, blending the paint into the Step 7 layer.

Brush 2
Chinese White and
Lemon Yellow

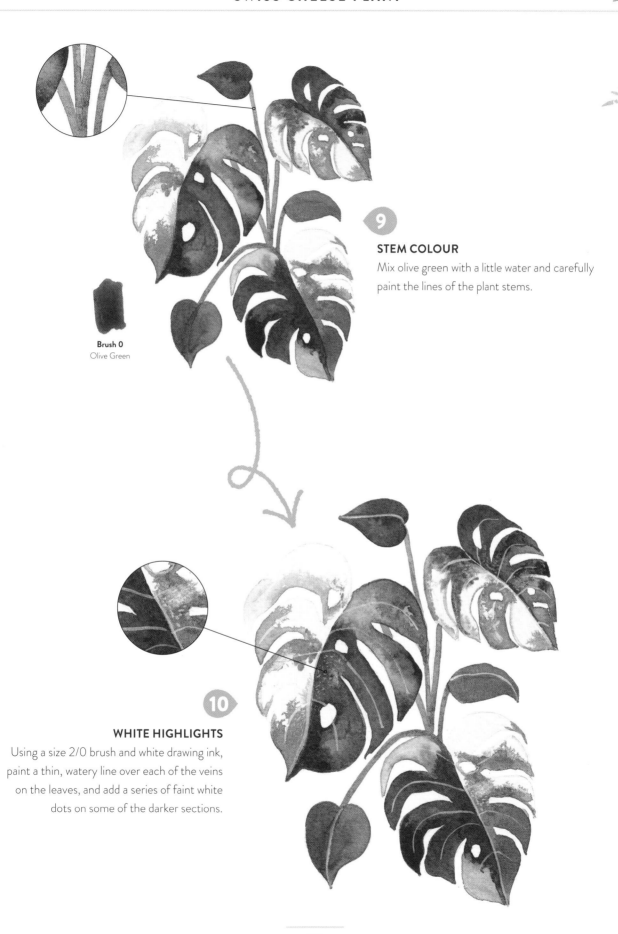

Brush 0
Olive Green

9 STEM COLOUR

Mix olive green with a little water and carefully paint the lines of the plant stems.

10 WHITE HIGHLIGHTS

Using a size 2/0 brush and white drawing ink, paint a thin, watery line over each of the veins on the leaves, and add a series of faint white dots on some of the darker sections.

DANDELION

Taraxacum officinale

Bright yellow dandelion heads dot lawns and roadside verges in the
summer months. Seen by some as a weed, this plant has many medicinal uses.

1 BASIC FORM

Using light pencil strokes, and following the
proportions and positions in my sketch, draw a
series of shapes that capture the plant's basic
form. For reference, my sketch is 16.5cm tall
by 12.5cm wide (6½in x 5in), with the largest
circle measuring 7cm (2¾in) across.

2 REFINED OUTLINE

Sketch a more accurate outline within your
basic shapes. Draw two flowers face on and
the third in profile. Notice how all the leaves
and flowers have ragged edges. Once happy
with your outline, erase the basic shapes.

3

PENCIL DETAILS

Using the final image as a reference, draw in the finer detail inside the face-on flowers, tracing each of the petals. Draw two layers of petals on the flower in profile. Go over the lines once more, pressing hard to create an indent to use as a border for the paint.

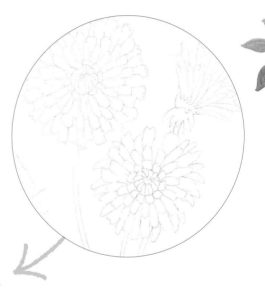

4

PENCIL IMPRESSION

Erase the pencil lines, leaving just the indent. If you prefer to keep a few marks, make sure you are happy for them to show through the paint.

Brush 2
Aureolin

5

FIRST WASH

Mix aureolin with lots of water and paint each of the flowers. Start from the centre in each case – or the base in the case of the profile flower – and add water to push the paint to the edges.

6

SECOND WASH

Mix a watery yellow ochre and paint the centre and innermost round of petals on each flower. Switch to a size 1 brush to paint the outermost round of petals. Mix a concentrated Winsor yellow, Winsor orange and yellow ochre and trace the indents of the second round of petals from the centre, blending the colour in with water.

Brush 2 & 1
Yellow Ochre

Brush 2/0
Winsor Yellow,
Winsor Orange,
Yellow Ochre

Brush 2/0
Aureolin

Brush 2/0
Raw Umber

Brush 2/0
Raw Umber and
Winsor Orange

7

BUILDING COLOUR

Using aureolin and a little water, draw a line along the left side of each petal in the third round, and on the outer petals of the profile flower. Mix a watery raw umber to paint the base of each petal on the outer round. Add a tiny drop of Winsor orange to the mix and paint the top edge of some petals, before washing with water.

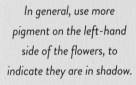

In general, use more pigment on the left-hand side of the flowers, to indicate they are in shadow.

Brush 1
Raw Umber

Brush 2
Olive Green

8

LEAF AND STEM COLOUR

Mix raw umber with plenty of water to paint the three stems. Mix olive green with lots of water and paint all of the leaves.

Brush 2
Winsor Yellow, Winsor
Orange, Yellow Ochre

Brush 0 & **2/0**
Olive Green,
Raw Umber,
Permanent Sap Green

9

CREATING DEPTH

Add lots of water to the darker Step 6 mix and sweep a wash over the left side of each flower. Add raw umber and permanent sap green to the leaf colour. Trace the central vein on each leaf and brush the colour up and out to the left. Add plenty more water to paint the right side of each leaf and some thin lines over the leaf base of the profile flower. Switch to the size 2/0 brush to paint short, thin, watery lines on the left side of each stem.

10

WHITE HIGHLIGHTS

Using white drawing ink and the size 2/0 brush, paint white highlights over the petals. Starting with the central bud, draw lines radiating inwards and a series of dots around the outside as a border. Add lots of water to draw highlights on each petal on the right side of each flower.

PASSIONFLOWER
Passiflora caerulea

This exotic-looking flower is native to the tropics of South America.
It is admired for its delicate fringe of bright blue and white filaments.

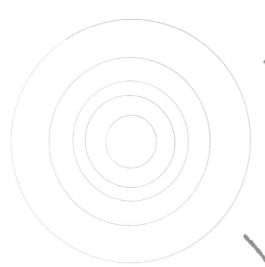

1

BASIC FORM

Working lightly with a pencil, draw a circle roughly 12cm (4¾in) in diameter. Use a compass if you'd like to be neat. Draw four inner circles at roughly even intervals, with the smallest around 1.5cm (⅔in) in diameter.

2

REFINED OUTLINE

Sketch a more accurate outline within your basic shapes. Draw out ten long, pointed petals, making the finished flower shape 14cm (5½in) in diameter. At the centre of the flower, note that five stamens radiate out in a rough star shape, with three overlapping styles above them. Once happy with your outline, erase the basic shapes.

3

PENCIL DETAILS

Using the final image as a reference, draw the finer details, including the long filaments, divided into sections. Add the tendril at the bottom right of the flower. Go over the lines once more, pressing hard to create an indent to use as a border for the paint.

4

PENCIL IMPRESSION

Erase the pencil lines, leaving just the indent. If you prefer to keep a few marks, make sure you are happy for them to show through the paint.

Paint each petal from the tip down, brushing the paint between the filament indents. This way, you are less likely to become confused over which parts of the flower need painting.

5

PETAL COLOUR

Mix lemon yellow with viridian, a few drops of permanent sap green and lots of water. Paint each petal with a watery layer of this colour. Do not worry if you go over the filament indents here and there.

Brush 1
Lemon Yellow,
Viridian, Permanent
Sap Green

6

FLOWER CENTRE

Add plenty of Winsor yellow to the petal colour and paint a layer at the centre of the flower. Take care to avoid the other elements in this crowded area.

Brush 0
Lemon Yellow, Viridian, Permanent Sap Green, Winsor Yellow

Brush 1 & 2/0
Lemon Yellow, Viridian, Permanent Sap Green, Winsor Yellow

Brush 2/0
Aureolin

7

STAMENS AND PETALS

Add more sap green to the Step 6 mix. Paint the stamens and the tips of the petals on the left of the flower. Switch to the size 2/0 brush and use a more concentrated green along the left edge of each stamen. Mix a concentrated aureolin and dab a rough line around each anther to suggest a hint of pollen.

When painting the purple elements, add slightly more pigment on the left side of the flower than on the right, as this is in shadow. You can also dab the paint on the right side for a paler finish.

8

BUILDING COLOUR

Paint a watery aureolin at the centre of the flower. Mix permanent rose, permanent alizarin crimson and indigo to paint the styles; a series of strokes radiating out over the yellow centre; and the surrounding circle of dots. Add a drop more indigo and paint the lower section of each filament.

Brush 2
Aureolin

Brush 0
Permanent Rose, Permanent Alizarin Crimson, Indigo

Brush 0
Permanent Rose, Permanent Alizarin Crimson, Indigo

9 FILAMENTS

Mix cerulean blue and French ultramarine with plenty of water, and add a few drops of Windsor violet and permanent rose to create a bluey purple. Paint the top section of each filament. Add lots more water and switch to the size 2/0 brush to outline the middle section of each filament. This should be very thin and not contain too much pigment.

Brush 0 & 2/0
Cerulean Blue, French Ultramarine, Windsor Violet, Permanent Rose

You can add a white highlight down the central (white) section of each filament, although this might not be necessary if your paper is already white enough.

10 FINISHING TOUCHES

Use white drawing ink and a size 2/0 brush to add highlights around the central section of the flower and on the tips of the petals. Add some water to the Step 7 green and paint the tendril emerging from beneath the flower.

Brush 0
Lemon Yellow, Viridian, Permanent Sap Green, Winsor Yellow

CHRYSANTHEMUM

Chrysanthemum 'Spider'

With its head of fine, tubular petals, this chrysanthemum presents a challenging prospect for the watercolour artist – the perfect final project to test your skill.

1

BASIC FORM
Using light pencil strokes, and following the proportions and positions in my sketch, draw a series of shapes that capture the bloom's basic form. For reference, my sketch is 18cm tall by 14cm wide (7in x 5½in), with the largest oval measuring 10cm x 8cm (4in x 3in).

2

REFINED OUTLINE
Sketch a more accurate outline within your basic shapes. Draw out rough flowers with lots of intricate petal lines. Draw in the stem and some long, flowing leaves. Add detail within the leaf shapes. Once happy with your outline, erase the basic shapes.

3

PENCIL DETAILS

Using the final image as a reference, draw each central bud of short, thin petals curving upwards, with longer petals radiating in all directions. Go over the lines once more, pressing hard to create an indent to use as a border for the paint.

4

PENCIL IMPRESSION

Erase the pencil lines, leaving just the indent. If you prefer to keep a few marks, make sure you are happy for them to show through the paint.

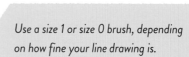

Use a size 1 or size 0 brush, depending on how fine your line drawing is.

Brush 1 or **0**
Permanent Rose
and Yellow Ochre

5

FIRST WASH

Mix a watery peach using permanent rose and yellow ochre and paint all of the petals. You should be able to see the indents through this layer. Paint from the tip of each petal and flow the paint inwards to avoid becoming confused over where to paint.

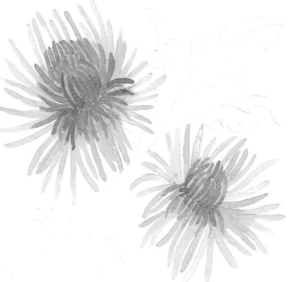

Brush 0
Permanent Rose,
Yellow Ochre,
Burnt Sienna

6 SECOND WASH

Mix burnt sienna into the peach mix, and carefully paint over the shortest petals to the front of each flower. Leave a very thin border between the upward- and downward-curving petals. Allow to dry before painting the shortest petals to the rear of each flower.

Brush 2/0
Burnt Sienna, Yellow
Ochre, Burnt Umber

Brush 0
Burnt Sienna, Yellow
Ochre, Burnt Umber,
Winsor Orange

7 CREATING DEPTH

Mix an opaque burnt sienna, yellow ochre and burnt umber. Paint fine lines around the short petals and a concentrated colour at the top of the central crown. With a clean brush, use the Step 5 colour to paint a thin, watery line down the left side of each long petal. Add Winsor orange and paint a watery layer over the middle petals.

8 LEAF AND STEM COLOUR

Mix a concentrated olive green and paint the left side of each leaf and the stem. Allow this to dry, then add more water and paint the right side of each leaf, creating a two-tone effect. Use a more concentrated colour where the leaf stalks meet the plant stem.

Brush 2, 0 & 1
Olive Green

Brush 0
Olive Green
and Indigo

9 LEAF AND STEM DETAIL

Mix some indigo with the olive green and use plenty of water to blend a series of small, horizontal shadow lines down the left side of the stem. Trace the central vein on each leaf section. Add plenty more water to your brush and wash a small amount of this green over the base of the leaf where it joins the stem, flowing the paint up the leaf slightly.

10 WHITE HIGHLIGHTS

Using white drawing ink and a size 2/0 brush, apply a thin white line down the right side of each central petal. Adding lots of water to the white, paint lines down the right side of each leaf section, blending them out slightly.

RESOURCES

ART MATERIALS

CASS ART
cassart.co.uk
I purchase the majority of my painting equipment from the art shop Cass Art. The watercolour paper, paint set, drawing inks and paintbrushes used in this book were all purchased from Cass Art. Their blog is also very insightful!

WINSOR & NEWTON
winsornewton.com/uk/education/guides
The paint palette I use is the Winsor & Newton Professional Watercolour set. The Winsor & Newton website is very useful and has a range of great guides.

INSPIRATION

NATURE GUIDES
I love collecting vintage scientific guides on British flora. A personal favourite is the Observer's book series, published by Frederick Warne & Co, and available in a huge range of titles. I often find these beautifully illustrated nature guides in vintage shops, charity shops or on eBay.

BOTANICAL DRAWINGS
A long-standing tradition has seen artists producing detailed botanical drawings for scientific study. Their drawings and paintings are works of art in their own right and I like to draw on them for inspiration.
A personal favourite is Harriet de Winton's *New Botanical Painting*, published by Ilex Press in 2019.

FURTHER READING

Baines, Valerie, *Classic Sketchbook: Botanicals*, Rockport Publishers, 2017.

Birch, Helen, *Just Add Watercolour*, White Lion Publishing, 2019.

Lighthipe, Mindy, *The Art of Botanical & Bird Illustration*, Walter Foster, 2018.

Pedder-Smith, Rachel, *The Watercolour Art Pad: Flowers*, Mitchell Beazley, 2017.

Putt, Katie, *Boost Your Watercolour Confidence*, Search Press, 2021.

Woodin, Mary, *10 Step Drawing: Flowers*, Search Press, 2018.

Woodin, Mary, *10 Step Drawing: Nature*, Search Press, 2020.

INDEX

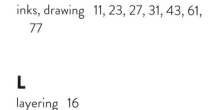

ABOUT THE AUTHOR

Eleanor Longhurst is a professional creative living in Bristol. She has run the illustrative nature-inspired brand Little Paisley Designs since 2014, and works from her sunny, plant-filled home studio, assisted by a needy cat and fuelled by lots of cups of tea! This book is a culmination of years spent painting flora and fauna and a wish to share her love of watercolours and plant life!

AUTHOR ACKNOWLEDGEMENTS

For my lovely auntie, forever my number one fan, you would have been so proud to see this book.

To my parents and sister for their unwavering support, for encouraging me to start my own business, always helping as unpaid interns, and tolerating a huge amount of stock lying around the house in those early days. Without you none of this would have been possible!

To my indie business girl gang – the Christmas Ruiners – for always having my back, pepping me up, and for the constant crisp chat.

Thank you.